CW00858637

TWICE
SURREAL

TWICE SURREAL

A Memoir of

World War II and Korea

Stuart Gardner Hunt

TWICE SURREAL

Copyright © 2005 by Stuart G. Hunt.

ISBN-13: 978-0-557-25278-7

DEDICATION

To my wife, *Edith Bridget*

To my daughters,
Patricia Anne   Susan Stuart
Caroline Helen

To my grandchildren,
John Stuart   Susannah Kristine
Matthew Tilden   Genevieve Noelle

To my great-grandchildren,
Cooper Stuart   Spencer John

For all servicemen and women,
living and deceased,
who have fought so gallantly.

ACKNOWLEDGMENTS

Without the encouragement of my daughters this book would not have been written. Its publication would not have been possible without my editor, my eldest daughter, Patricia Anne Hunt. Patricia put in countless hours researching, editing, and improving my English, for which I offer heartfelt thanks. I am grateful to Susan Stuart Hunt, my middle daughter, for her work on the graphic design and layout, and for being the go-to person in completing the publishing process. My youngest, Caroline Helen Gamma, provided unstinting support throughout the project.

Many thanks to my friend Albert Wallace, who was one of my roommates in Stalag Luft III. He was able to locate and send me a copy of the report on the forced marches. This enabled me to confirm dates and specific locations. The report Al sent was signed by D.E.L.Wilson G/Capt., Senior British Officer.

CONTENTS

AUTHOR'S NOTE

The title of this book, *Twice Surreal*, was chosen for the following reasons. When a person enters military service his lifestyle is completely changed. First, you have given up freedom, in the sense you are not in a position to make your own decisions. Your life is in the hands of others. You do not make the decisions; they are made for you. It does not matter if you agree, because you do not have the right to disagree. Others control you. Your life is for sale. You are told where to go, what you are to do. You are disciplined to obey.

Many men and women want to live this life. In time of war, numerous people can't wait to enlist. But I am sure that, for many, after they see the horror of war, the enthusiasm wears thin, or disappears.

I myself was one of those eager young people, ready to go fight for our country, willing to accept that my life was a number, disposable on the cheap, and not to question. But when the war was over my reflections centered more on the waste of humanity than on the glory. On my second experience of war, in Korea, I was not as gung ho. I had seen the horror of war. My thinking was more on doing the time and returning home to my family. There is no glory in war, and often enough you have to experience it to understand that fully.

THE EARLY YEARS

─────────────────────────────────

The depression years were very hard on most families and the Hunt family was no exception. We were always on the edge of financial disaster. In Canada, as in the United States, everyone had to work to support the family. My dad had many jobs, mostly short term. My mother worked as a telephone operator for the water and power company. My brother and I delivered papers mornings and afternoons in summer and winter. The winters in Montreal are very cold. I had to ride a bicycle ten miles round trip, often in ice or snow, because my route was so spread out.

My brother Tom (older by fifteen months) and I started paper routes at about age nine or ten. Many times we would have to go out and make collections in advance because the family needed a few dollars for food. We were a happy family, however, and we did not feel put upon. My brother and I were always well dressed; I don't know how Mother and Dad were able to do it.

TWICE SURREAL

In those early years in Montreal, during heavy snowstorms the city would require people to shovel snow down the manholes in the street. My uncle, Jim Hunt, who worked for the city was in charge of giving brass rings out to the ones selected to work. Even though my brother and I were only about thirteen or fourteen, he would see that we got on the work force. We worked at the same place all the time, the corner of Dorchester and Guy Streets. Wow! It must have been the coldest corner in all of Montreal; with the wind howling the wind chill would be forty to fifty degrees below zero. We usually worked all night.

The trucks would dump the snow and we would shovel it into the sewer manhole. Sometimes we would get a job in the daytime. My brother found the work degrading and would always turn his head when a bus passed for fear that some of his friends would see him. Of course, when we worked days we missed school, but the work never lasted more than two days at a time. Our favorite food at a break was at a restaurant where they served beans on toast and hot tea, named Northeastern Lunch; I will never forget the name. I still love beans on toast. We were paid eleven cents per hour.

As kids hockey was our whole life. It seems as though we started to skate as soon as we could walk. We played on hockey teams starting at age six. We would skate all night when the sleet would freeze on the pavement. We would walk ten miles round trip to watch the Montreal Canadiens and other teams play. My brother and I were into all sports, including softball and lacrosse; I was also on the school swim team.

In 1938, my father and a partner by the name of Wally Watt opened a flying school at an airfield located near Cornwall, Ontario. My father purchased two aircraft for the purpose of flight instructions. The school did fairly well in the beginning. I learned to fly and things were looking better for our family. My father had plans for me to attend The Royal Military College of Canada in Kingston, Ontario. In fact, Dad sent a deposit for my entry the following year. I was thrilled at the prospect, and was looking forward to a military career in the Royal Canadian Air Force. But this was not to be.

Watt was the company's treasurer and, to make a long story short, he embezzled the money and the project failed. Our family had to file for bankruptcy. The creditors came to our house and removed all our possessions, even our bikes, and sold them to pay outstanding debts. It was not long after that we left Verdun (Montreal), and moved to the city of Ottawa, Ontario, the capital of Canada.

In Ottawa we rented a house in an area called Westboro. The house was very nice, but I have no idea where the money came from. In any case, the war had started in Europe. 1940 was my last year of high school. With the shortage of manpower and the need for defense workers I was enrolled in a tech school, Ottawa Tech.

This school taught sheet metal and other trades that would help the war effort. You went to school for four hours and then you went to work in the factory making parts for aircraft that were being used in Great Britain. We were paid *five cents* per hour. After three months we got *ten* cents, and I got my high school diploma.

My dad in the meantime was a flier and was an inspector at an aircraft plant named Ottawa Car. He called the family together and said, "Boys, you are making *fifteen cents an hour*. My boys are worth a lot more, so we are going to Toronto to work for Canadian Car and Aircraft in Malton, just outside of Toronto. You are worth at least *forty-five cents per hour*." So off we went to

5

Toronto. We were hired immediately at fifty-five cents per hour at the Malton aircraft plant. Later we moved on to Hamilton, Ontario, and worked in a plant at sixty-five cents per hour.

In the meantime, my dad was in touch with a number of aircraft plants in the United States and got an offer to test fly for Ryan Aeronautical in San Diego, California. He filed the necessary papers at the US Immigration Office in Toronto and we were off to the promised land, California.

My brother elected to stay behind at this time, so just the three of us, Dad, Mother, and Stuart, along with the two cats, took off with a small trailer behind the car across the USA. A lot of funny things happened on this trip, cheap motels and lousy food, but we were in good spirits and finally made it to San Diego.

We landed in San Diego with maybe forty dollars between us. We stayed the first night at the Plaza Hotel on Fourth Ave at Broadway. The next day we were able to find a house on Shirley Ann Place in the University Heights neighborhood. With the rent deposit, we were left without enough money to turn the water on. The Baxter family, who lived next door, used their hose to fill the bathtub with water for cooking and drinking, and we showered at their home. My dad got an advance after the first week and then we were home free. This was around August 1941; I was eighteen. The following week I got a job as an inspector in the machine shop at Ryan. My previous experience was very helpful and I think I got about *eighty-five cents* per hour. That was an excellent wage at the time.

Things went well in San Diego. My brother Tom and my good friend Lloyd Stuart joined us. I was interested in meeting some local friends. I met a guy down at a bowling hall, where I was playing snooker. He told me he was going to San Diego State College. I said, "Yeah, well you must know a few of the girls out there."

He told me about a pretty blond that impressed him. He did not know her personally, but her name was in the school directory. I took down the information. The phone number must have been listed in the book. I called her home and her mother answered. I told her that I was new in town and that I would like to meet her daughter. She said that she had three. I asked to see Bridget. She said, "If you want to meet my daughter, you will have to meet me first." So I made arrangements to come by and that's how I met Bridget Darsey.

We started to date, nothing serious. We would go on car rides; you could do that then, as San Diego was a small city of just over 200,000 people. There were no freeways and the drive up to Lake Hodges was very serene and pleasant. Sometimes Lloyd would come with us. Lloyd was not an American citizen and could not work in the defense plants. Instead, he got a job teaching sheet metal at a trade school, which worked out well, as all war plants needed skilled trades. Graduating students were hired immediately.

Bridget at the time was working late shift at the telephone company. I would drive downtown to pick her up. She got off work at 12:30 am. and I did not want her out alone waiting for the bus at night. Buses were available around the clock because the defense plants were working twenty-four hours a day. We used to go to the drive-ins for a malt and then I would take her home.

Meanwhile, my family was carefree. My mother worked at Marston's, a top department store in downtown San Diego. She worked in the china department, because she loved nice English bone china and glass. Things were improving.

7

TWICE SURREAL

We, the boys, had a lot of fun in San Diego. We bought an old Chevrolet car. Being typical boys, we cut the roof off and made it a touring car. We spent a lot of time at the beaches, which I might add were not crowded like today. Bridget and I used to go over to Coronado a lot and dance to the big band music. We also would go to the Palladium in Los Angeles and dance to the music of the big name bands names like Tommy Dorsey, Glenn Miller, and so forth. It was quite a drive up to LA in the early 1940s. When you left the red roofs of San Clemente, there was nothing but orange groves.

Drive-ins were all the rage for fast food. Bridget and I would always have a malted milk shake before I took her home. Yes, they were fun years. Girls wore saddle oxfords, sweaters, and skirts. Boys wore shirts with dress pants and shoes. Not Levis and tennis shoes. No long hair, everyone was clean cut, and jitterbug was the dance. It was very romantic to take the ferry across the bay to Coronado. They were fun years and San Diego was the playground.

Then one day I was over in Coronado sailing with a friend when someone shouted to us, "The Japs have bombed Pearl Harbor." At first it simply did not register. We knew about the war in Europe and the Battle of Britain of course. Now we were at war, too. All young men had to register for the draft. It was only about a month later that the Army Air Force called my dad into service as a captain. Meanwhile, I was trying to join the Flying Tigers, based in China, but had no luck. I went down to Lindbergh Field to enlist at the Air Force recruiting office. They told me that they were not taking applications for flight school without two years of college. I was so damned mad I called the Canadian Consulate in Los Angeles and asked them if the Royal Canadian Air Force wanted any fliers. Their answer was, "When can you leave?"

Meanwhile, my father was in Wichita, Kansas, and was soon to be transferred to Willow Run, a B-24 plant outside of Detroit. He was to ferry B-24s overseas, with a wartime unit known as the ferry command. So the family was separating. The Hunt family would never be together as a unit after 1941.

So in about May of 1942 I left for Ottawa (at the expense of the Canadian government) to enter the RCAF. Bridget and I had talked about my going. We did not have any commitment—we were quite young—and we parted with "see you later." I did take a four by eight picture of her. It was always placed in sight until I was shot down. I really don't think she was in love with me at that time.

I remember the trip to Ottawa, as it took about twenty-four hours to get there. I think the plane stopped at every airport between here and there. I was to report for the physical the day after I arrived. I believe I stayed with my mom's sister, my aunt Binnie, the next few days while I was taking physicals and tests to see if I was a real person. During this time I was of course out with some of my old friends, as we had previously lived in Ottawa. Dancing at the Trocadero down on the riverfront was great.

This is a photograph of Bridget Darsey taken in 1940. I carried this picture with me to the U.K. Bridget and I were married upon my return in 1946.

AIRCREW TRAINING

Once in Ottawa, I managed to pass the medical exam (joke) and was inducted into the RCAF. This was in September, 1942, I believe, and I was shipped to the Manning Pool in Lachine, on the outskirts of Montreal. You can imagine—here I was, back in my own back yard, and they told me that I was not able to leave the post for six weeks. Well, I decided that I was going to work around this ruling. I wanted to see my best friends, especially Forrest Donaldson, my sidekick in our younger years.

So boot camp, as it is known in the US, consisted of shots and uniforms and being shouted at, more shots etc. In the meantime I was trying to figure out how I was going to get out of this prison. There was a lot of snow, which did not make for good reconnaissance of the area. I did, however, notice at the corner of the compound that I could climb the fence without being seen. So after bed check at 9 pm. I would get dressed and head out to my escape area and over the fence, with the knowledge that I would have to be back before morning light.

It was great; I would catch a streetcar and head into the city. Everyone knew that I should not be out of camp. The hair on our heads was shaved close, and therefore I was a dead ringer for a new recruit. Somehow I did not give a damn. The walk from where I climbed over the fence and walked through the deep snow was very exhausting, and the return trip was worse. I had to figure at least an hour to get out and back in.

With all that, it was still fun, with one exception. Unfortunately, Forrie had already been posted overseas. I never got to see him again; he was killed on flying operations over Europe.

Forrest Donaldson was my very best friend in my younger years; we played hockey on the same teams. We grew up and played hockey together on school teams, and with the midget and juvenile hockey leagues. We also played for the Montreal Canadiens Junior Club. You would have to be a hockey player to know the thrill of playing hockey in the Montreal Forum. I will never forget that moment; it was every Canadian kid's dream, and I made it. At the time, of course, I didn't know the fate of my friend, and blithely played cat and mouse, in and out, the entire time I was in boot camp and luckily got never caught.

Next we were shipped to Ottawa for tarmac duty, at Uplands Airport. This is duty at the air station doing whatever came up—servicing planes, parking planes, taxiing planes—while waiting for assignment to the next aircrew class. So this was all right; I knew a lot about Ottawa, having lived there, and had plenty of friends. I had duty warming up the aircraft. Ottawa can be very cold and there were bitter cold days of forty below zero. I had other duties like working in the officers' mess tending bar, which was better than tarmac duty. In any case, we had the unpleasant duties that are all part of the drill, while waiting for assignment to cadet training.

Finally, I was posted to the University of Toronto for a refresher course. It was mostly math and Morse code, as well as other courses pertinent to training as aircrew. While attending the university I met Jim Horwood. We both had parents in Detroit; his had lived there for quite some time. We became close friends and remain so to this day.

We had a lot of good times in Toronto, especially at the pub at the Royal York Hotel. We had the same problem here as in boot camp—bed check was at ten o'clock. So we would have to sneak out after the check. It was tough since we were on the second floor and had to climb down a rope we had hidden in the room. Then we would have one of the guys pull the rope back up and on our return, let it down at two in the morning.

Well, sometimes the rope would not be there. We would have to wake someone by throwing small pebbles at a window and then get that person to go wake the person who was supposed to drop the rope. Meanwhile, air force police patrolled the area. Get the picture? Somehow we were never caught. And I was surprised to finish the refresher course at the university in the top five. I don't remember studying, but I must have.

Anyway, we were off to our next station to start cadet training at Trenton, Ontario. Before reporting, we had a week's leave. Jim and I took the train to Detroit to see our families.

Life at Trenton Air Base was uneventful. The only thing that stands out is that they had boxing tournaments. Naturally, I was the one who had to get in the ring and represent our class. It was quite hilarious. Jim was my second and instead of water between rounds he would give me a bottle of beer. Three three-minute rounds and that was enough to really tire you out. Then we would go celebrate at the station beer hall.

We were stationed at Trenton a couple of months, really a drag—mostly ground school, and some flying. Upon graduation we were posted to Portage la Prairie, Manitoba, fifty miles west of Winnipeg. At this station we would complete our training. If you did not meet the required proficiency, you washed out, with no second chance. Before posting, however, we had a seventy-two hour pass, so Jim and I went to Detroit for a short visit.

We had a long train trip from Toronto. The first two weeks in Manitoba were quite a change. The countryside is very flat and flying revealed the vast amount of lakes in the area. I had never traveled this far west in Canada before. Shortly after our arrival we received a forty-eight hour pass. Jim and I were off to Winnipeg by train.

Winnipeg was dry, so we had to find a speakeasy. I remember that the owner treated us like royalty. To make the story short, we ended up in a cheap hotel. We were a little under the weather in the morning. I looked at my watch and realized we had missed the train that we needed to take to make our training flight. Well, if you are AWOL, and late for your flight lesson, you were in big trouble. We took the next train that put us back at noon, four hours late.

We were immediately taken into custody and had our hats taken and the buttons removed from our uniforms. Then we were brought before the adjutant. I thought they were going to put us in the stockade. It is quite comical now, but at the time it was very serious. I thought this would be the end of my air force career and that I would get a year in the cooler. After we told our story, however, lying of course, we were censured and confined to base for the balance of our training. In addition, we had extra duty, working every night in the sergeants' mess, serving food and doing KP. I thought, there goes my chance for a promotion to pilot officer.

So the balance of the training was miserable for Jim and me but we always laughed a lot. Graduation came and the 152 still in the class were given their wings. We were graded collectively on all previous and present training. I finished third in the class of 152, with a grade of 94.4. I never could figure that out, but I felt confident that I would receive a commission to pilot officer. As I was an American, and wore USA on my shoulder, I thought that they would be more inclined to the Canadians, even though I was born in Montreal. All but three of our class graduated as sergeants. I graduated as a pilot officer. We were then given leave, about ten days I believe. So back to Detroit I went.

About two days after arriving in Detroit, I received a telegram confirming my commission. I was to go to Windsor, Ontario, across the river from Detroit, take the government authorization to a clothier of my choice, and purchase my officer's uniforms. Of course I was delighted, although I was disappointed that Jim did not get a commission.

During the ten days leave I also received a letter with orders to report to Halifax, Nova Scotia, for embarkation to the European Theatre. With tears, and my mother hugging me, I boarded the train that would take me to Montreal. After a brief stay in Montreal, we were on to Halifax. We boarded the troop train; many of the airmen were guys I trained with. They had their fun with me, saluting and calling me "sir".

Jim was a sergeant and I was a pilot officer so we were separated in Halifax. In the harbor was the liner Queen Mary, our transportation to the UK. Meanwhile, we had about a week in Halifax. Jim said that the food was not so good in the enlisted men's mess. So I said, "Hey, guy, wear one of my uniforms and eat with us in the officers' mess." So that is what we did. Of course, that would have been a court martial for sure had we been caught! Since there were so many troops in Halifax, I doubt that anyone would have known except for other airmen that had trained with us. In any case, nothing ever came of it. It is interesting to note that when I was sworn in as an officer in Halifax, I did not have to pledge allegiance to the King; if I had, I would have lost my American citizenship.

The day came when we were to board the Queen Mary. My quarters were excellent since I was an officer; we were four in a private stateroom. It was my understanding that there were 21,000 troops aboard the Queen Mary—Army, Navy, and Air Force.

We were to cross the ocean without escort. The Queen Mary was fast enough to perform a zigzag pattern at speeds of thirty knots. At the time there was not a submarine that could travel that fast, which is what the powers-that-be relied on. It was, however, a nerve-racking trip. A torpedo travels at approximately twenty-five knots; one shot at us from an angle would have created the biggest disaster of the war. The Queen Mary had levelers, but nothing for pitch, so when the bow dug in the spray would come well over the front part of the ship. I had been assigned a duty watch, usually at night, to walk the decks and to be sure that no one was smoking as we were under complete blackout.

Feeding 21,000 troops is a massive job, requiring round the clock feeding, providing two meals per day. It was hell down in the lower decks—sweating bodies, packed in like sardines. They rotated the troops from the hellhole to the decks every day. The best part was that it only took us three and half days to cross the Atlantic Ocean. We docked in the Glasgow, Scotland area. I do not remember the name of the port.

I remember the day we disembarked in the spring of 1943. It was cold and rainy, typical Scottish weather. We went from the ship to waiting trains. The train took us to Bournemouth, on the south coast of England. This is where all Canadian aircrews assembled for assignment to various training stations.

Bournemouth is a beautiful seaside city—very charming and I fell in love with it. During my stay, I met a number of my old friends from Canada, who were waiting for posting to training stations. Many of the airmen were from Verdun, Quebec, where as children, we grew up together.

The disappointing part was that I missed Forrest Donaldson by one week. I never saw Forrie again. He was killed in a raid over Europe and is buried in Holland. His plane was shot down and all the crew were killed I was told. What a waste of young life. He was truly a gifted athlete and a hockey trophy is named after him in Quebec. Little did I know at this time that many of my classmates and friends would never survive this war. The fact is that less than half of our class survived.

In Bournemouth, I was billeted in a private home. All the houses in the area during the war were taken over by the British government. The families remained in their homes, but all spare bedrooms were used for the RCAF. Food was not provided in these homes; we had a combined mess in town, but slept and bathed there. The families were very cooperative and I am sure they were well reimbursed by the government.

I had an opportunity, as there was a shortage, to buy some Royal Dalton china for my mother and mail it to her. It is interesting to note that because of the way we were brought up most of my comrades sent a portion of our military pay to our parents, as I did. This was later to prove a windfall for me, one that I did not expect.

So Jim and I were parted at Bournemouth. He was an enlisted sergeant, so we ate and slept in different quarters. We spent time together, however, and did have an enjoyable time in the city.

My first station in the United Kingdom was close to the village named Wellsbourne, just a few miles from the Shakespeare town of Stratford-upon-Avon. The airfield was a conversion unit, training in twin engine Wellingtons. It was at this station that airmen met with each other to find compatibility and form a flying crew. This is where I met and formed our crew. My favorite was the mid-upper gunner, whose name was Pat Draper. Pat was big strong man, a farmer by trade. He was married with a couple of children. I had the opportunity to visit with Pat and family after the war in Kingston, Ontario, where he had his farm. He died shortly after; cancer got him. He was part of my life, and I miss him. He was the type of person who was always there in time of need. We still hear from his son at Christmas time. He had five or six children.

The other crewmembers were David Stubbs, the bombardier; John Wells, the pilot; Hugh Mooney, the navigator, and Graham Walker, the wireless operator. All were airmen with a specialty that makes up a bomber crew. Moreover, the question was, could we live with each other and function as a unit? We all trained in different sections. Stubbs and I were the only officers in this crew at the time. Later, the other Canadians were promoted to officer rank. The Brits, Walker and the engineer, whose name escapes me, remained sergeants.

Jim Horwood was also posted to Wellsbourne, and we would get together at odd times at the local pubs. The officers had valets called batswomen. They would make our beds and shine our shoes. Really, the Brits never give up on amenities. We had some wild times down at the Kings Head, the local pub. Most of us had bikes and I can tell you that riding a bike in the rain, drunk, you find yourself in the ditches full of mud. I remember trying to keep the bike on course, but I always ended up in a ditch. It made a lot of work for the WAAF who had to clean my uniforms. Therefore, I spent a lot of my pay on giving tips to WAAF (Women's Auxiliary Air Force) personnel. We also spent leisure time in Stratford. There is a river, the Avon, which runs through the town. It played host to a lot of our young airmen, who tried navigating a straight line on their bikes while being tipsy.

Oh, yes, one thing that I should note, as this will come up later. When returning from a night at the local pub, for some reason I would be singing Irving Berlin's song, "Marie" (the Benny Goodman version where the background singers are singing "I'm Living in a Great Big Way", which was another popular song at the time). When I entered the BOQ (bachelor officers' quarters), I would immediately go to Officer Anderson's bed; he would be asleep. I would smack him on the ass and shout, "Living in a great big way!" He would always answer, "Hunt, for Christ's sake! Go to bed!"

Our first indoctrination air raid was made from Wellsbourne; it was a leaflet raid over the city of Ville St. George in France. I know I was very nervous, as we had no fighter escort, and it was a night mission. As it turned out, all the missions I flew were conducted at night. I remember wondering on this raid if I was going to get the chop dropping leaflets. The trip went okay with one exception. An aircraft was detected, which alerted the squawk box, a radio beam that tells you another plane is within 500 feet and closing. The closer it gets the faster the beeps. We were unable to tell if it was an enemy plane or not, so we took evasive action. This was accomplished by turning and diving into the direction of the attacking plane, then recover and repeat. This is also known as the corkscrew maneuver. This is great maneuver in the daytime, but at night you were very lucky to spot the plane before it had fired on you.

The station commander was DFC (Distinguished Flying Cross) British RAF, whose rank was wing commander. I remember the welcome he gave us. As we gathered for briefing he said something to this effect. "Don't get any ideas that you are needed. Any person enlisted or otherwise who does not salute a superior officer will be dealt with accordingly." What an introduction! But that was the British for you; they still think they won the war by themselves. He also informed the officers that a contracting a venereal disease would be a court martial offense. Hell, with the amount of saltpeter they were putting in the food I don't think there was any danger of that happening. So with all the saluting, saltpeter, and training we were ready to move on.

There were a number of interesting events that come to mind that happened at Wellsbourne. One night coming back from a leaflet raid, the pilot I was flying with—we were on a training mission—landed the plane so hard that the tail wheel broke the iron drainage cover on the runway. It drove the tail wheel up through the rear fuselage, barely missing the rear gunner. I thought that was very exciting and promised not to fly with that wacko again. Another time an aircraft taxiing ahead of us allowed his brakes to get too hot. The result was that he taxied into the plane ahead of his. The propellers acted like a buzz saw and removed the tail section from the fuselage of the aircraft. Well, this was too much for me as I could not control my laughter and had to shut down. Can you imagine the crew in that plane looking back down the fuselage and there was a new exit? Luckily, it was not a Halifax or the rear gunner would have been hamburger. The plane was a small twin Beechcraft which the commanding officer of the station used, which made it all the more hilarious, as he was the consummate British snob.

I received a week's pass and Jim and I were off to London. We stayed at the Strand Palace, a hotel in Piccadilly. London was in a complete black out and I can tell you it was black. In the fog and drizzling rain, you had to feel along the sides of the building on the sidewalk to navigate. We would find a pub, and then finding our way back to the hotel was a major undertaking. We were in a bar during a bombing by the Germans. When the sirens sounded, all the patrons headed for the shelters. Jim and I stayed, no kidding. We were the only ones in the place and just helped ourselves to whatever suited our fancy. As the all clear sounded we left quietly. I don't know exactly how quietly—quite bombed would be more accurate. Then the fun began, getting back to the hotel, which was only blocks away, but in a black drizzly night it could take hours.

On one of our trips, as usual, we ran short of funds. There was an organization called Lady Elizabeth that found accommodations with families who would open their homes to guys on leave and provide a little atmosphere for the servicemen. They were private homes and some were large estates. On this particular occasion, we were sent to a family about thirty miles north of London. When we approached the address we were in awe, for it was not a home but a large estate. There were huge iron gates at the entry. The home was a massive castle-like structure with extensive grounds and was rather run down due to the lack of help. Sure enough this was the place.

The women of the house greeted us and showed us to our rooms. Well, the bedroom I was to occupy was large, almost the size of our entire present home. The bed had a canopy and was raised to a level of about five feet. There was a small stepladder that was needed to climb into the bed. The bed was down feathered and you just sank down. Wow! You left your shoes outside the door and they would be polished. The estate had tennis courts, fishing pond and many other amenities. The dining room was a large banquet hall; the dining table must have been thirty or forty feet long. We were served by one of the two servants who were available due to the war.

The master of this estate was some kind of titled aristocracy and owned a mercantile factory of some kind. Their son, who was eight or nine, had a playroom just for electric trains, all raised to waist level. The room was as large, maybe twenty by thirty, and full of working trains, like you have seen on display, only more.

They were very short of food, because everything was rationed, and we brought a few food items from the base. The granite house was massive, very ornate; I would guess 20,000-plus square feet. We stayed two or three days and then returned to the base.

After Wellsbourne, the next station was a British commando unit. Their job was to train us in the art of survival and escape. Jim Horwood's crew was also posted here at the same time, as well as other aircrews. We were billeted as a crew in the same Quonset hut as Jim's crew. Each hut slept two crews, fourteen men.

The training was for two weeks. The first week was instruction in the art of self-defense. In other words how to kill and live. These instructors were mean and they treated us like the enemy, which was the purpose of the school. We were prisoners and it was up to us to try to escape. They also taught us how to land when bailing out of an aircraft in a parachute. They used a sixty-foot tall tower and a lower one of about twelve feet where you jumped and were taught how to roll on impact.

The second week we were taken out in the woods and told we had to live off the land and evade capture for five days. I don't think it stopped raining the entire five days, as I was wet going and when it was over. We were given a commando knife, a compass, a Smith and Wesson .45 revolver, a map, and pills to purify water. These things were what we would have on our person when we would be on flying operations.

We were dropped off individually at different locations. With a "good luck" from the instructor you were on your own. I had no idea where we were as we were taken to locations, blindfolded, in a covered truck and dumped. We were not to take the blindfold off until we no longer heard the truck. Jim had been sitting next to me in the truck and he got off two stops before I did. So after I was deposited I saw the tracks of the truck and knew which way by sound that it had departed. I therefore assumed that Jim would be in the opposite direction. I also reasoned that I would have to stay off the tracks of the truck, as that would be the obvious way to track back. Our guns had blanks in them and if you fired at one of the enemy before they did, you were still in the so-called game. The commandos did not consider this a game, however.

Five days of evading, I thought, how do I do this? By chance I saw some wild berries and collected about two handfuls that I put in my soft leather helmet and then in the pocket of my flying suit. We were all wearing flying suits, as this would be the way we would be shot down. I took a reading with my compass of the direction of the truck tracks, not knowing how many circles the truck made before dropping me off. Nighttime was approaching; the drizzle was constant. I left the area and looked for a place to spend the night. I found heavy brush and wiggled my way in to spend the night, being careful not the break any branches. The night passed very slowly. I thought about the draft notice I had received in Wellsbourne from the US Army. This gave me a laugh, and I thought, well, come and get me. I was a long way from San Diego.

As dawn broke, the mist was heavy. I thought I would travel parallel to the truck tracks, keeping about one or two hundred feet away in the heavy brush. About mid-afternoon I thought I saw a movement and ducked into the brush and lay quiet. Peering through the rough, lo and behold, I saw Jim. I called over to him, quietly, and beckoned him to join me. We bickered back and forth as to the best action to take, and decided to remain at this location and try to build a shelter to keep us a little drier. We decided to stay put for the next two days and nights. That way we would only have one night left, and then we would then make a move to try and find the camp.

We spotted some more berries and at night we collected enough to keep us from real hunger. We were able to catch enough water coming off the leaves to satisfy our thirst. It was constant drizzle. On the fourth night, which would become the fifth day, we decided that we should take a chance on the truck tracks and head north with hopes of locating the camp. We were pretty beat by this time. The berries gave us dysentery and our water supply was not plentiful. Suddenly, we came upon a barbed wire fence and decided this must be the camp. We lay low until daybreak and sure enough, not 500 feet in front of us was our own Quonset hut. We scrambled under the wire and were making a dash for our hut, when from a foxhole a commando popped up and nailed us. We were short by 150 feet. We felt good after we were told that we were the last to be captured. All the others had been captured. This training proved to be very important to me in surviving what was to come. We all graduated and received a three day pass. We went into the city of Leeds for a wild weekend.

My next station was to another conversion unit, converting to four engine bombers, namely the Halifax. The Lancaster, a sister bomber, was the better aircraft. The British left the Halifaxes for the Canadians. The Halifax was powered by four 1400 horsepower Merlins in the initial models, and was capable of speeds of 250 miles per hour, hardly a record breaker. Altitude was around 21,000 to 22,000, making it the lowest level of the planes that would be flying on sorties over Europe. All other bombers would be flying at a higher altitude. Do you start to get the picture? We were indeed cannon fodder. In any event, that was our lot and there was no turning back.

Our training at Topcliff Airport was intense. We flew tactical maneuvers and cross-country navigation trips and had gunnery and wireless training. Training included aircraft recognition and a refresher course in the use of Morse code.

Everything was suddenly more serious to all of us now. We started to feel apprehensive and we became more critical of each other's mistakes. For the first time I suppose it became apparent that we were just a few weeks away from reality and that the next step was not going to be a baby step. We completed training and were now supposed to be a finely tuned machine, capable of carrying "bombs" to blow the hell out of so-called military targets. We knew, of course, that indeed we had been placed in the role of the executioner. This was later to prove true. It was no different for the thousands who were dying under the nightly German air raids on London and many other English cities. Bomber command called this "area bombing" of military targets.

We completed this phase and were given a forty-eight hour pass with instructions that we would be assigned to a squadron on our return to base. Jim was still with me, with a different crew, but we knew that it would be unlikely that we would be assigned to the same squadron. In any event, we had a good time in the town of Huddersfield in Yorkshire. One of the crew had relatives there, so it was pleasant. Returning to the base I was informed that we were to report to the 425 Squadron, the French Canadian Alouette Squadron. The airport was in a small, unknown village named Tholethorpe. Even today if you ask a person where Tholethorpe is, they shake their heads, never heard of it, and they may live within a few miles of it. We have experienced this in recent visits. Tholethrope is located about twenty miles NNW of the City of York, in Yorkshire. The 6th group consisted of six Canadian bomber squadrons, all located within a radius of about thirty miles in Yorkshire.

Jim's crew was sent to the 420 Squadron located thirty or thirty-five miles north. "The Snowy Owl" squadron was stationed at the Teesdale airport near Darlington. That was to be the last time I saw him until the war ended.

This photo was taken of me at age 19 when I was attending aircrew studies, at the University of Toronto, Ontario in 1942 prior to flight training.

This picture shows three yanks in the Royal Canadian Air Force.

Left to right: Roger Villeau, Jim Horwood, and me.

We were attending the RCAF Aircrew Training in Trenton, Ontario, Canada in 1942.

I am pictured here in my flight suit at the RCAF Aircrew Training in Trenton, Ontario, Canada in 1942.

Another picture with my mates at the RCAF Aircrew Training in Trenton, Ontario, Canada in 1942.

I am on the top right and my best friend, Jim Horwood is on the top left.

I graduated as a Royal Canadian Air Force Pilot Officer. This is the graduating class in Branson, Manitoba in June 1943.

Age 20, this is my RCAF Pilot Officer graduation photograph taken in 1943.

Pilot Officer James A. Horwood, went through training with me. Jim and crew were shot down over the North Sea and had to ditch. Fortunately they were picked up by Dutch fishermen and were hidden in a farmhouse until liberated by allied forces. Jim and I remained lifetime friends.

THE BOMBING MISSIONS

Tholethorpe, January 1944, was a very small village. There were maybe fourteen houses, a tiny post office that also sold a few eatables. There was of course the pub named "The New Inn". Other than that there was only the airfield and the supporting base buildings. Our BOQ was down the road from the pub about one-third mile. It was rather pretty and the countryside was very flat, ideal for aircraft use. There were twenty planes to a squadron. There were two squadrons at this airport.

Upon arrival at the station, Stubbs and I were assigned to the officers' quarters. We were the only officers in the crew at the time, so Stubbs and I shared a room. The officers' mess was very close and the food was what was available, like eggs and Brussels sprouts for breakfast, some kind of chopped up meat or sausage and Brussels sprouts for lunch and dinner. Get the message? There was a small confectionery on the side of the road that sold candy bars and soda, similar to Kool-Aid, rotten stuff. Any charges in the officers' mess, for beer etc., were put on a tab and automatically taken out of your pay. So you had to be careful that you did not drink too much or you would not have any pay for the month. Our pay was deposited into the Royal Bank of Canada in London. When you wrote a check you had to be sure there were sufficient funds, that it would not bounce, for that, my friend, would have been very bad news for an officer in the RAF.

So here we were at the crossroads, the pay back for all the money they had spent training us. A cohesive aircrew of seven who were to take the 60,000 pounds of metal and explosives and transport it through intense enemy flak and enemy fighters, find the target, and blow whatever to hell. That is presuming we hit the target in the first place, which I will explain later.

We were assigned a Halifax Mark II. The call letter was "L", so we called her "Lucky Lady Love". We had a pair of legs painted on the fuselage and the ground crew was formed for "our" plane. Even though we were assigned to this plane, other aircrews flew it when we were on leave or on other assignments.

We flew a few more training trips, cross-country, for navigational purposes. Then the alert came. On our first mission into Germany we were all very nervous. My, my, how the stomach tightens up. Many thoughts run through your mind: Are we ready for this? How will we perform? God, I hope we hit the target! God, I hope we get to the target! Why do I feel so nervous? Later it was apparent that this is a normal human feeling. Prior to this, we had only been on "two-nickel raids", as they were called, to France in the Wellington twin-engine bomber.

All bomber air raids by the British and other allied air forces were flown at night, with exception the last months of the war. The U.S. flew daylight with fighter escort. We had no fighter protection and did not fly in tight formation. We flew in waves, usually four. The ideal was to be in the second or third wave. The first and last wave suffered the most casualties. All my missions were flown at night.

The target was Frankfurt on the Rhine and in the briefing we were given the weather conditions, the color of the markers that marked the target, where we were to drop our bombs, and other pertinent information. What areas to expect heavy flak, search light locations, areas of heavy German fighter activity, which was everywhere as far as I was concerned.

The Germans had radar and were able to transmit to their fighters in the bomber streams. They were excellent pilots and had the advantage at night by being able to spot the red exhaust manifolds of our bombers. We had dampers on the exhausts, but you could still see the glows. The Germans shot down most of our planes by attacking us from the underside. We did not at this time have a mid-under gunner. Later in the newer Mark III Halifax, a fixed free 50-caliber machine gun was put in to help this situation.

Frankfurt was about a six and a half hour round trip. After the briefing we would have an early dinner and then head out to the plane. While waiting for takeoff the crew joked around, acting brave. I don't know exactly what load we were carrying but probably around eight tons— something like one 2000 pound, eight 500 pound, and the rest incinerator canisters. Also we carried bales of tin foil. This was thrown out of the aircraft to confuse the German radar along the target route. Usually the engineer got that job. On this trip we had an extra passenger, an OSS (Office of Strategic Services) agent, who at a designated spot parachuted out of the aircraft to do whatever. He never spoke to us, when our navigator pushed the green light in the main body of the aircraft he was gone. All that was left was the teeter cord that opened his chute.

Just before dusk the first flare was fired, and that was the signal to get into our planes. Everyone would check in; the second flare meant to start taxiing into position for takeoff. All the planes would be in line waiting for the green flare to begin takeoff. As each plane took off we would climb to altitude of 10,000 feet and rendezvous over the North Sea. Then, at the appointed time, we would climb to the assigned altitude, which was between 18,000 and 20,000 feet. As luck would have it, we were in the first wave. As I looked around and saw all these planes, my first thought was that it was a wonder we didn't collide. That did happen but very rarely.

Night vision was extremely important, as you can imagine. At best you could not see another aircraft until it was upon you, unless it was silhouetted against the white clouds or a reflection off the moon. That meant 200 to 300 feet in normal conditions, so the gunners had to react very quickly to determine that if the intruder was theirs or ours. If he saw that the aircraft was the enemy, he would order the pilot into a tactical maneuver, called curve of pursuit. It's a corkscrew action that turns the plane into the attacking plane, thereby reducing the enemy's ability to get the nose of his aircraft into firing position. This maneuver was practiced a lot in training.

We had another aid, which was a radio beam that sent out a signal in a 360-degree arc from the tail of the plane. If the beam hit any metal, it would come back as a beep. The closer the oncoming plane was, the faster the beeps. The problem was that you never knew the exact location, up, down, or on the sides.

The terrifying moment was when the beeping

stopped. With the Germans, that usually meant that the fighter was under us, but since the radio beam became ineffective when another aircraft passed ninety degrees in any direction, it could also be to the side or above us. Whenever that happened, you immediately went into a corkscrew maneuver.

So, it was our first real mission deep into Germany. We waited in line as the eighteen or nineteen Halifaxes laden with destruction took off in one-minute increments. When we got a green light, we taxied onto the runway and lined up on the center line. Full brakes, full throttle, the engines were screaming, the brakes were released, and the plane lurched forward desperately trying to gain speed. The runway got shorter and the tail wheel lifted. You pulled back on the yoke—the plane wants to stay on the ground, you pull harder and finally, like a hippo laboring to get out of the mud, we were airborne, barely clearing the fence at the end of the runway. (Many Halifaxes plowed into the farmer's field during take-off, making a beautiful gouge through his crops.)

We headed for Robin Hood's Bay for rendezvous. Hundreds of aircraft were circling and at the appointed time we headed for Germany. Usually our route was not direct, since we tried to confuse the Germans. Also, there were diversion and support flights to further try and confuse the German fighter command. As we crossed the North Sea, you suddenly realized how alone you were. Gone were familiar surroundings. No "Hi, Bob!" or "Hey, Joe." It was just you and a straining monster trying to gain altitude, carrying death and destruction.

As we crossed the coast of Holland we were in radio silence, with the exception of intercom within the plane, used only when necessary. The outside temperature was thirty to sixty degrees below zero. We had "heated suits" that worked most of the time, but any portion of your flying suit that was stretched, like over the knees, got very cold.

The night raid on Frankfurt consisted of 816 aircraft—620 Lancasters, 184 Halifaxes, and twelve Mosquitoes. Our route did confuse the Germans for some time. Only a few of their fighters found the bomber stream. Thirty-three aircraft—twenty-six Lancasters and seven Halifaxes were lost, four per cent of the force; thirty-three aircraft with seven airmen each equaled 231 airmen missing. The ratio for survivors was one in seven. Therefore, of the 231, possibly thirty-three were able to get out of the aircraft by parachute and might be alive or taken prisoner. Little did I realize at the time that I would be a visitor in the near future to this city, as a prisoner of war.

Reports show that the city was hit very hard. Half the city was without gas, water, and electricity for a long period. There was severe damage to the industrial area. The report also had a long list of historic buildings, churches, and hospitals destroyed. 948 people were killed, 346 seriously injured, and 120,000 were bombed out of their homes or businesses.

One result of these heavy raids was that captured airmen often had to be protected by their German guards from the assaults of angry civilians when they passed through Frankfurt to reach the nearby Oberursel interrogation and transit camp. I personally had this experience in this city. If it had not been for the German guards, I would have been dead or maimed.

The inward trip was uneventful other than we had one attack over the target by a German fighter. He made one pass and went on to another target. The flak was so thick approaching the target that you could have walked on it. Searchlights surrounded the city and the scene was unbelievable. You were in the spotlight. Many of our aircraft were visible, fighters darting around like flies after a sugar bowl. It was so bright you could read the small print on a cigarette package. The city below was a floral array of color from the coded color markers dropped by the pathfinder force, indicating the target, and the fires started from the thousands of incendiary sticks dropped. It was the worst and most fateful blow of the war to Frankfurt, a blow that simply ended the existence of the city of Frankfurt—a city that had existed since the middle ages.

Our flight back was without incident and we landed exhausted about 3 am. After debriefing, we hit the sack and were told we would be flying again that night.

I shall not go through every raid but I will hit the ones that are burned in history. Remember Britain was being pounded as well. Every night as we flew to Europe the Germans were reciprocating. In fact, on more than one occasion we would witness the flashes from the bombs bursting on an English city in the distance, as we climbed to rendezvous for a mission.

Now we were veterans—piece of cake. Funny how one successful raid can give you an uncertain confidence. Of course, we needed it, and the crew, like all others, felt it would never happen to us. The reality of it all was that it wasn't *if* it would happen, but *when*.

The mission for that night was cancelled early allowing us the go into the city of York. The base motor pool would supply trucks to take us in. We were also told that midnight was the last return. Well, we missed many and would have to find a bike, or by chance an army truck that would be going close to the base. We would have to walk six miles from that drop off.

York was fun. The main attraction was Betty's Bar. The bar was about thirty feet long and had a full mirror on the bar wall. The owner had an electric pen; we were then permitted to write our names on the mirror. Thousands of names were inscribed. On a trip back a few years ago, we found the bar was gone and had been replaced with a tearoom. They still had a few pieces of the mirror around a post downstairs, but most of the mirror had been broken or destroyed.

We also frequented a dance ballroom, the type with a mirror ball in the center of the floor revolving around and causing wacko light reflections. Well, there usually were many fights as the men outnumbered the women maybe ten to one. You can imagine the problems.

I don't remember how I got back that night, probably Sgt. Pat Draper, our crew's mid-upper gunner, got me home. This was typical of our time off. The local pub, London, or York, depending on the amount of leave we had.

I remember the next day, March 24, 1944. We were told that tonight's mission was on and briefing was at 1400 hours. As the briefing began, the commanding officer of the station announced, "Gentlemen, this is a big one. Berlin." You could have heard a pin drop, then murmurs and whispers. Hell, the last time they had gone to Berlin we got our asses kicked. Nevertheless the briefing went on: route, weather, cloud cover, diversions, and flight altitude. The aircraft would be heavy with fuel and bomb load. One thing I will say about the British— they must have put a huge bomb on the ground and then built a plane around it. There was no armor protection for any of the crew. The Americans had flak suits and armor plating in the cockpit. The flight would take about seven and a half hours—a long time when you could never let your guard down.

We assembled as usual, got into the plane, and waited our turn for takeoff. Gross weight of the Halifax is around 66,000 pounds. I am certain we were closer to 71 or 72,000. I thought for sure that the plane would never leave the ground. It wouldn't have either if it had not been for gusting winds of up to twenty knots. Winds like that can be dangerous but somehow we lifted off.

The bomber group with 811 aircraft was dispatched to the raid on Berlin. 577 Lancasters, 216 Halifaxes, eighteen Mosquitoes. We lost seventy-two aircraft: forty-four Lancasters and 28 Halifaxes lost—8.9 per cent of the force. Yes, seventy-two aircraft downed by flak and fighters. 518 were airmen missing. Approximately seventy-four would make it to become POWs or to be hospitalized with severe wounds.

Let me explain this snafu. The night became known in bomber command as "the night of the strong winds". A powerful wind from the north carried the bombers south at every stage of the flight. Not only was the wind not forecast accurately, but also it was so strong that methods to warn crews of the changes failed to detect the full strength of it. The bomber stream became very scattered and radar-predicted flak batteries at many places scored successes.

Think of Berlin as a coliseum. There were two circles of searchlights around the city, the outer and the inner. The space between the circles was approximately two miles. As you crossed the rim of the outer lights, flak batteries would be constantly firing into this area. The flak was so thick that the fragments from the exploding shells would hit the fuselage of the aircraft with sounds like tin cans tied behind a newlyweds' car.

Meanwhile, the city was a mass of flames and our color markers were blown every which way due to the strong winds. When you made it through the flak corridor you were in the center of the arena, like gladiators in the Roman coliseum. There were Jerry fighters flashing by

43

and tracer bullets flying in every direction. On all sides you saw aircraft bursting into flames and occasionally exploding. We finally dropped our bombs. That bomb run seemed like a lifetime. When 8,000 to 10,000 pounds of bombs are released, the plane shoots up about 200 feet. The next trick was to get the hell out of there, but of course you had to fly through the flak corridor again.

The return trip was a nightmare for some, as the planes were so scattered that part of the force even strayed over the Rohr defenses. It is believed that approximately fifty of the seventy-two planes were lost to flak batteries, the remainder to attack by night fighters.

The bombing was so terrible that 126 small towns and villages outside Berlin recorded bombs and thirty people were killed in those places. No industrial buildings were reported destroyed, but some were damaged. They claimed that five military establishments were badly hit. Approximately 150 people were killed and 20,000 were bombed out.

This was the last major RAF raid on Berlin during the war, although the city would be bombed many times by small forces of Mosquitoes. For us the homeward trip was uneventful; we had had enough for one night. On landing we found large holes in the tail section of the plane, probably from flak. We had one fighter attack over Berlin, but our mid-upper gunner was able to change the fighter's mind. It was a long trip and we were ready for some sack time, which of course came after debriefing. The lives we lost because of this weather snafu were a waste of boys at war.

Little notes: visibility at night was suspect at best. The enemies were moonlight and searchlights. It takes over thirty minutes to regain night vision when exposed to bright light. Our friend was darkness, clouds, and altitude. Wearing an oxygen mask for six to nine hours could be very annoying. Your face gets chapped and sore, and the zero weather adds to the discomfort. People have asked me about what you do when you need to urinate. Well, it was a pain because of the flying gear we were wearing, but there were relief tubes in the plane. Many times, however, in critical situations, airmen were known to have voided in their flight suits due to nerves.

Two nights later we hit Essen with 705 aircraft—476 Lancasters, 207 Halifaxes, twenty-two Mosquitoes. The sudden switch by bomber command to a Rohr target, just across the German frontier, caught the German fighter controllers by surprise and only nine aircraft—six Lancasters and three Halifaxes—were lost.

The city of Essen was covered by cloud, but the Oboe Mosquitoes marked the target well. This was a successful attack. Forty-eight industrial buildings were seriously damaged, 1,756 houses destroyed. 545 people were killed and 1,570 were injured. A large number killed were labor forces in German factories.

The operation took five and a half hours. We referred to a short trip like this as a milk run, but nevertheless, if you were one of the nine aircraft that did not return, then you bought the farm no matter how short or long. One advantage of being shot down over Holland or Belgium, if there was an advantage, was that you would be closer to friendlier people and the possibility of getting help more easily, certainly better than Germany.

Then there was Kiel, where thirty-three aircraft were lost and Hamburg with thirty-eight lost. We just kept on going and gaining more confidence with each trip.

March 30, 1944, was one to remember. There was a full moon and we were sure we would not fly that night. Normally this would be a stand down for the main force. But on the basis of an early forecast, there would be protective high cloud cover on the outward route, when the moon would be up. They stated that the target area would be clear, however. It is known that a Mosquito carried out a reconnaissance and reported that the protective cloud cover was unlikely, and instead there would be cloud cover over the target. But the raid was not cancelled.

795 aircraft were dispatched—572 Lancasters, 214 Halifaxes, and nine Mosquitoes. Nuremberg would be a seven and a half hour trip. Eighty-two bombers were lost on the outward route near the target.

The German controller ignored all the diversions and assembled his fighters at two radio beacons that happened to be astride the route to Nuremberg. The first fighters appeared before the bombers reached the Belgian border and a fierce battle in the moonlight lasted for the next hour. The action was much reduced on the return flight, when most of the German fighters had to land, but *ninety-five* bombers were lost in all, sixty-four Lancasters and thirty-one Halifaxes, 11.9 per cent of the force dispatched. *This was the biggest bomber loss of the war.*

Again the winds were poorly forecast. Bomber crews claimed they bombed Nuremberg, but approximately 120 had bombed Schweinfurt, which was fifty miles northwest of Nuremberg. This mistake was a result of badly forecast winds causing navigational difficulties. Two Pathfinder aircraft dropped markers at Schweinfurt. Most missed the target and it was reported that only two people were killed in that area. We bombed the wrong target.

The main raid on Nuremberg was a failure. The city was covered with thick cloud and a fierce crosswind, making the final approach difficult. Markers were too far to the east and a ten-mile creep-back developed into the countryside north of Nuremberg. Both Pathfinders and bombers were under heavy attack throughout the raid.

Little damage was caused in Nuremberg; sixty-nine people were killed in the city and surrounding villages.

So even with information that was given to British Air Force Command by the reconnaissance Mosquitoes that the conditions were not suitable, they sent us, knowing that we would not have cloud cover. They knew this, and by their stupidity 685 young warriors were reported missing; of those, 590 would be killed and 95 would be taken prisoners.

We were badly shot up and had to make a forced landing at an American airfield. The landing gear would not come down and we had to belly land the plane. It veered off the runway and crashed into a hanger. Fortunately a fire did not break out and we all managed to escape with minor bruises. We were picked up the next day by one of our aircraft from the squadron. They had us as missing for about six hours.

The next trip was a walk, three hours and fifty-five minutes, Ghent, Belgium. This was a Group 6-only raid and included 122 Halifaxes and ten Pathfinder Mosquitoes. My understanding was that no aircraft were lost. Ghent was the only target of this night to provide a report. The raid caused much damage at the Merelbeke, Melle railway yards, on the main road to Brussels. The surrounding housing area was also hit. 428 Belgians were killed and 300 injured. 584 buildings were destroyed, including seven schools, two convents, and an orphanage. 1,009 other buildings were damaged.

It was often the case that the papers reported no aircraft lost. We noticed many times how the losses were downplayed; I suppose this was the keep the morale up for the people, as the Germans continued to bomb England. We never knew what the official count of losses was. Soon there would be the German V-1 "Buzz Bombs" that were launched from coastal batteries to pound English cities.

We had few days off and I don't remember what I did. Perhaps I played hockey. I played on the RCAF hockey team whenever I could. We played in Birmingham. I only did this occasionally as I rarely had that kind of time off.

I'm pictured here (left) with Bombardier F/O David Stubbs. It was taken in 1944. I was 21 years old.

We are standing next to a Halifax II in Tholthorpe, England where the 425 Squadron was stationed.

The twin engine Wellington bombers were used for training and conversion to multi-engine.

We flew two missions over France, before transfer to the four engine Halifax bomber.

Pictured is the Halifax Mark II taken at the conversion unit at Topcliff airport in Yorkshire England.

We were converted from the Wellington Bomber to the Halifax MKII bomber.

This unknown crew is pictured with the Halifax Mark III. Note the under turret which was a new addition to the Halifax..

I was shot down in a similar Halifax Mark III.

Nuremberg Is Smashed By British, Canadians At Cost of 96 Planes

R.C.A.F. Loses 13 Ships as Great Armada Pours Death and Destruction on Germany

London, March 31.—(AP)—A great armada of R.A.F. and R.C.A.F. bombers numbering probably more than 1,000 smashed at the southern German transport centre and Nazi congress city of Nuremberg and other points in the Reich last night at a cost of 96 planes—the heaviest toll ever taken of an Allied air fleet in a single operation. The R.C.A.F. —which made a big contribution to the blistering attack— lost 13 bombers. The Canadian bomber group loss was five less than the record of 18 lost by the R.C.A.F. in the heavy attack on Leipzig on the night of February 19-20. Thirteen R.C.A.F. bombers also were missing after the last heavy night attack on Berlin on March 24-25. The record R.A.F. loss was announced just as the entire German network with the exception of Vienna in Austria shut down this morning shortly after the warning that "enemy planes are approaching."

Great Bomb Load

The first German warnings said the daylight raiders were over Hessen-Nassau province in Prussia in which Frankfurt is situated.

The announced loss last night, which contrasted to German claims of having inflicted the greatest defeat of the war on the R.A.F. with the shooting down of 132 four-engined bombers, was incurred in the 17th heavy bomber operation in March by the R.A.F.'s sky fleets.

The brief Air Ministry communique made no reference to the bomb load, but it used the term "in very great strength," suggesting that probably 2,000 long tons of bombs were dropped, despite the distance involved.

Are Unescorted

Unprotected by shields of escorting fighters such as guard American daylight formations and only lightly armed, the big R.A.F. and R.C.A.F. bombers fell easy prey to Nazi night fighter pilots and anti-aircraft gun crews, who could silhouette them against the moonlit sky.

The big air battle of the night swirled over Germany and occupied territory during almost the entire 1,100-mile round trip between Britain and Nuremberg, with an average of one bomber plummeting to earth every 11 miles. Nearly 700 airmen were believed to have been killed or captured.

Our plane was in the second of four waves of bombers. Flying at night we never had a fighter escort. The loss of 96 planes was the highest ever recorded for a single raid.

The winds were very strong that night and the sky clear. It was a perfect night for German night fighters. It is my understanding that a few German pilots became aces in one night.

SHOT DOWN

While on this leave we were called back to the station for a mission. It was April 24, 1944. I had only just turned twenty-one on April 5th. It was a rather strange day for me. I was not feeling good about this trip. I had a very uneasy feeling in my stomach. I was unable to pin it down, as usually I would be considering it just another trip.

It is amazing how your mind can cause your whole being, body, and thinking to react in an unnatural way. I always envisioned a bomber as a huge bomb that they built an aircraft around. In reality this is correct. The Halifax like its brothers was built to carry bombs to destroy the enemy. We were a flying explosive with wings.

One indication that this was not going to be a good day was that Pilot Officer David Stubbs, our bombardier, reported ill. He and I shared the same room, as we were the only officers at the time. We were very superstitious. When one of the crew was not flying, a substitute would replace him. I was very disturbed even though he was replaced by the squadron bomb leader named Flight Lieutenant Charles Maddin.

Another disturbing indication was that our own Mark II Halifax was lost and we had a new plane, a Halifax Mark III with radial engines. You might think that this is not a problem, except the change is viewed as a bad omen.

I packed all my belongings in my quarters and told Stubbs if something happened not to send my clothes to the Air Force storage. I gave him the address of a Mrs. Jenkins, an aunt of one of my fellow flyers. I instructed him to have my belongings sent to her home. I also wrote a letter to my parents telling them that if I were shot down that my belongings would be at this address. My parents corresponded with the Jenkinses and a pen pal relationship remained for many years. My family sent many care parcels to the Jenkins family.

At briefing we were told the target would be Karlsruhe, with 637 aircraft—369 Lancasters, 259 Halifaxes, and nine Mosquitoes. They reported nineteen aircraft missing, but I later found that it was more like thirty-three. The report shows eleven Lancasters and eight Halifaxes lost, three percent of the force.

Our own plane, "Lucky Lady Love", had been lost on the previous raid. We had to ferry a new Mark III Halifax to Tholethorpe for the night's raid. The Mark III had radial engines and also had a fixed 50-caliber machine gun in the underside of the plane. So, that night we flew with the station bombardier to replace the sick Stubbs and extra gunner, which made a crew of eight. I don't know what the problem was, but I was not comfortable.

The flight started about nine o'clock, about a five hour trip. The new plane preformed well; the Mark III had a little more horsepower. We lifted off nicely and did the usual with rendezvous and the new headings were given by the navigator. Our flight altitude was 18,000 and it was cold, bitter cold, and ice was forming on the leading edges of the wings and nose of the aircraft. The ice would break off and hit the sides of the fuselage with drum-like sounds, very nerve wracking. We climbed another 1,000 feet to see if we could get out of the icing. It seemed to work for a while. The next problem was from the engineer, who announced, "Hey, Skipper, we are going to have a fuel problem. These engines are eating up the fuel and we will be lucky to make it back."

The reply was, "Okay. We are not far from the target area, so after the bomb run we will cut out one engine on our return trip. That should do it, right?"

"Yeah, I think so," the engineer answered.

Next the navigator: "Hey, Skipper, we are about five minutes early. You are going to have to dogleg to waste time." On this raid there were approximately 637 planes. We were usually separated in four waves and we were to be in the second wave.

The skipper answered, "For Christ's sake! Are there any more surprises for me? Give me a heading."

So we doglegged for two and a half minutes south, made a 180, and returned to the flight path. Well, this was as bad as it gets. Rejoining a stream of hundreds of bombers at night was a very dangerous maneuver as it set you up as a stray for enemy fighters; you don't want to be a one on one. You want to be one in a hundred; the odds are much better. In addition, coming back into the main flight path of hundreds of other aircraft does not make for a good day.

We were back in the main stream; the wind was bad, icing began again. "Bogie, bogie," screamed a gunner. "Corkscrew port!" The plane went into a violent left bank and on pull up the g-forces would drive you into your seat. We finally got back on the bomb run. "Bombardier. Target markers ahead, Skipper."

"Okay. You have the ship," was the reply. So it goes like this: the bombardier controlled the plane, he opened bomb door and then, "Bombs away."

According to the report I managed to get at a later date, there was cloud cover over the target and strong wind, which pushed the Pathfinders too far north and spoiled this attack. Only the northern part of Karlsruhe was seriously damaged. Most of the bombs fell outside of the city. One report says twenty-three people were killed, 133 injured, and more than 900 houses destroyed or badly damaged. Another report listed 118 killed. Mannheim, thirty miles to the north, recorded a raid by approximately 100 planes on that night. Aircraft unable to find the main target also hit Darmstadt, Ludwigshafen, and Heidelberg.

"Bombs away" was music to our ears. The flak was very thick and you could hear it hitting the sides of the fuselage. To this point we had flak but no night fighters. The flak was exploding all around us and we managed to get out of the trap. We were heading home and reassessed the fuel problem. In order to make it to an airport in the U.K., we had to shut down one engine, which we did. We were now at a slower speed and we became a straggler, not part of the main bomber stream. We realized that before we could reach the coast of Belgium, we would lose the main force and become isolated. This is one circumstance you did not want ever to be in.

In order to increase our air speed, we started a slow descent to try and overtake the main stream. The fierce cross winds, however, were blowing us off track. The navigator was trying to correct. Our warning beeper started; there was an aircraft aft of us, and then silence. The mid-upper gunner screamed, "Corkscrew port!," This was a maneuver that we used to evade the guns of the fighter by flying directly toward him, but it was too late. Just as we were about to enter the corkscrew the German ME 110 night fighter fired his 20 mm cannons, which ripped into the cockpit. An explosion of metal and plexiglas shattered the air and the plane almost stopped from the impact of the twenty-millimeter shells ripping into the forward section of our aircraft. The two starboard motors burst into flames.

The order to "bail out" was given. The mid-under gunner was killed outright. A chute was put on him and he was pushed out of the plane. Shrapnel wounded Walker, the wireless operator, in his right leg and arm although I did not realize this at the time as he was able to abandon the aircraft with the crew.

Ordinarily I would have opened the turret doors, grasped my chute, swung to ninety degrees, and bailed out but I heard the skipper say he was badly wounded. I did not know how extensive the damage was to the plane. Being a pilot I thought I might still be able to fly it back to England. So instead of leaving from the rear, I made my way up to the cockpit through the smoke. When I saw the starboard engines engulfed in flames and knowing that the fuel tanks were also located on the wing next to the burning engines, I realized the plane could explode any second or start spinning out of control.

As I reached the cockpit, the noise from the air stream entering the broken windshield was deafening. The plane was still flying level. I reached across the injured pilot and switched the plane to autopilot in hopes of keeping it level a little while longer. The fear was that the plane might go into a spin and prevent exit due to centrifugal force.

The bombardier came into the stairwell and, shouting, asked if I thought the plane could be flown. With the noise, it was impossible to talk. I shouted back, "No!"

and motioned for him to bail out.

The skipper's right hand had been severely damaged and his chute was on his left. I grabbed it and clipped it on his parachute harness. I then realized I had to turn it around so that the parachute ring would be positioned for his good hand. We descended down to the front hatch and left the plane. Everyone was out, the plane still flying level at that moment. By now the flames had engulfed the whole plane.

Our parachutes were the chest type. I had a pair of tennis shoes tied to the harness of the parachute, because in order to exit as fast as possible, I had to unzip my flying boots so that I could slip out quickly. There were times that the big boots could get stuck, hence the tennis shoes tied to the chute.

In a split second, as I dangled my feet out the hatch and extended my hand across the opening to be sure my head would clear, I dropped, pushing out. I thought, this has not been a good day. This part is very vivid in my mind. As I ejected myself out the front hatch I was on my back. I clearly saw the underside of the plane and the tail wheel passing above me. Remember, I would be moving momentarily at the same speed as the plane. I would say my speed was still about 250 miles per hour.

I reached for the parachute ring and pulled it, releasing the chute. The silk came out and hit me in the face, the laces on the tennis shoes snapped, and then with a sudden jolt, the chute opened. The pain in my groin was intense; the harness dug onto my right groin area. I had opened the chute too soon at a high rate of speed. I should have been in free fall for at least ten seconds. I said to myself, "Why did I do that? I know better," but my next words were, "Thank God I am still alive."

It was very quiet, with light rain. I watched as the plane went into a tight spin until it hit the ground in a ball of flame. I thought, "I'm going to land on top of it." In reality it was more than a mile from me. I had no idea the altitude at which I had bailed out. At that moment, I realized that I was still holding the parachute ring in my hand. Irvine Parachute was giving twenty pounds to anyone who returned the ring, as this was most uncommon. Most who jumped dropped the ring when pulling. I thought about it and remember thinking, how am I going to collect? And with that I dropped the ring.

As I looked down I could make out the coastline, but my depth perception was hindered due to the darkness and weather. Seeing a shoreline, I inflated my Mae West and this increased the pain in the groin area. The parachute was swinging me uncontrollably. I grabbed one side to steady the chute and WHAM, I hit. I don't know how long I was unconscious, maybe a minute, maybe five, or maybe fifteen seconds.

As I came to, I realized that I was being dragged in the water face up. I was frantic, because I thought that someone was dragging me. Coming out of a stupor you are completely confused and it took seconds for me to realize that the chute was still fully open and acting like a sail and dragging me. I grabbed one side and collapsed the chute. As I did that my feet hit the bottom of the water I was in. I had no idea where I was except that I was off the coast of Holland or Belgium.

This is the location in Holland where our aircraft crashed after having been was shot down. The crew bailed out and we were scattered in the area. Two of us landed in water northwest of Antwerp.

HUNTED

———————————————————

I regained my senses and in looking around I could make out the dark shoreline. As I moved forward, suddenly the freezing water took hold. I had to get out of it; up to this time I had been unaware of how frigid the water was. As I made my way to shore that I estimated at 1000 feet away, the area became more marsh-like and there were patches of solid marsh above the level of the water. The more I looked at the shoreline the more confused I became as to what I was likely to encounter. So I decided to stay on one of these little marsh islands until dawn and then make decisions.

As the hours passed slowly I was concerned about my mother receiving a telegram that I was missing. I thought, I will try to concentrate and through some kind of mental telepathy I hoped to be able to transmit a thought wave that I was okay. I did this for what seemed like hours. Somehow I convinced myself that I'd get through.

Now to other problems. As I looked at the coastline I made out what I thought were bunkers all along the beach. With this imaginary thought I was naturally very concerned about Germans on the beach preparing for an invasion that was yet to come. Much to my surprise what looked like bunkers in the dark drizzle were indeed concrete tank barriers.

As dawn broke, I was able to reconnoiter the situation. I was about sixty feet from the actual beach. The tide was out so there were a lot of small pebbles and one-half to one pound smooth gray stones, worn smooth from the constant washing from the tides and sand. Inland from the rocky area was a sandy beach, which in turn was about forty feet away from grassy inclines about five feet high. My dilemma was, how do I get to the grass area? I would have to cross a beach that I was convinced had been laden with land mines. There was not a soul in sight; I had to make a move. I had to get off this beach as they were certainly out looking for us.

I decided that I would walk to the edge of the sandy area, and from there I would throw rocks across a path to the grassy incline. As I look back on this, it must have been a sight if anyone was watching—I would throw a rock and fall flat in case of an explosion. I continued to do this until I had what I thought was a safe direct line. With a "now or never" attitude, I ran across the beach, trying to step on the stones. I climbed up the bank and fell into a trench.

There was a maze of trenches stretching as far as the eye could see. Obviously the Germans were preparing for an invasion at some future date. As I sat there feeling good about the beach maneuver, I took stock of what I had. First and foremost, I was without shoes. I had in my possession an escape kit, which included a cloth map, a compass, water purification pills, and pills to give energy and keep you awake if necessary. I also had a commando knife and a Smith & Wesson .45 revolver.

64

Hunted

I took off my flying suit and that left me with my battle jacket, blue shirt and pants, and heavy socks. I had previously hidden my parachute in the marsh area. I took off my jacket and shirt, and put the battle jacket on next to my skin and my undergarment. I then put the blue shirt over the battle jacket. So can you visualize this—a tight shirt and no hat or shoes? I realized that I would stand out and would be picked up fast in this garb. I had to find shoes for sure and civilian clothes.

I was desperately trying to find my location. As I looked seaward I realized that I was not on the coast, but had landed in an estuary on the coast. The actual North Sea would be about a mile or less away. Looking at the map, I could not find this configuration of estuaries off the coast of Belgium. The reason for my confusion is that on the return trip we were supposed to be just north of Dunkirk.

As I was trying to get my bearings, I heard a train approaching and it passed me going north about 500 yards east of my position. So then I studied the map and the only place I saw a train track that close to the coast was northwest of Antwerp, Holland. Okay, so that is where I must be, I thought, so I went with it. As it turned out I was right and our plane was certainly way north of the intended track.

It was now daylight and as I looked to the southeast I saw farms. At the end of one field, there was a row of trees and shrubs, perhaps fifteen feet wide, separating two farm fields. No one was in sight so I headed for this area, as I wanted to hide my flying suit in the brush. I also needed to dry out a bit as the drizzle had stopped. I was temporarily hidden and I took off the heavy socks. My mother knitted these socks for me. They were very heavy wool and went over the knee. She made them to keep my knees warmer in the frigid weather while flying. I tried to wrap and tie them for protection around my shoeless feet. I was able to accordion the socks and with straps from my flying suit was able to have some protection.

While sitting there I heard a voice speaking loudly, a sound that resembled, "Giddy up" or whatever farmers say to their horses to get them moving. As I peered through the brush I saw a farmer plowing the field in a methodical manner. He would plow back and forth and at the east end he would only be about twenty feet from me. I watched him for a couple of trips, wondering if I should make contact. I approached the farmer and nearly scared him to death.

He turned ashen. I had a stick and drew the initials RAF on the ground. He screamed something and shook his head in fear and motioned me away. He took off with his horse cutting a new path diagonally towards the barn. It was obvious that he was very afraid of German reprisal. I thought, "This guy is going to turn me in." I gathered myself together and headed south, crossing fields and dikes. I came upon a narrow oiled road. There was a crater-like mound off the side of the road. I climbed up and then settled inside the concave to get out of sight.

I watched the road. The traffic was light—a couple of farm wagons, a couple on bikes. I still was not comfortable about making contact, since my first one was so unsuccessful. Then a motorcycle with sidecar drove by heading north, carrying two German soldiers. It was getting late, around 4 pm. by now and I did not want to spend the night there. I looked down the road and coming towards me was a postman on a bike. I showed myself and he motioned immediately for me to get down. He looked up and down the road and approached me. In broken English he said, "Pilot, you stay here; I come back." All aircrew were called pilot in Belgium. I decided that I would have to trust him and wait.

Hunted

It had been at least three hours since I had contact with the postman, and I became really nervous. Then I heard, "Pilot, come quickly." It took me by surprise; I had not seen or heard him approach. He walked ahead of me, like he did not want to be seen with me. I followed with a lot of apprehension. Here I was, possibly putting my life on the line with a complete stranger. I remember feeling the knife and the revolver and wondering if I would have to use them.

We approached a farmhouse. The postman—I guess it was he, as it was dark—motioned to me to go into the barn and wait. I opened the barn door and entered. There was a lantern flickering dimly, the only light. A voice in English from the loft said, "Up here." My heart was pounding; I had no idea what to expect. I climbed the ladder to the loft. The ladder was then pulled up.

To my surprise there were two other airmen. One told me he was a British RAF fighter pilot and the other an American airman. Both were still in uniform, but not full uniform, rather battle jacket and Ike jacket. I was very uncomfortable. My mind was still in shock, and the trauma of the escape so far had me very unsettled. Little talk was exchanged between us, as no one was sure of the other. This was fine with me. I needed to lie in the hay and warm up because I had nearly frozen laying out there waiting for the postman. The door of the barn opened; it was about 11:30 pm. A young boy called for the ladder. He brought me a hot tea that had brandy or something in it and a bowl of hot barley and potato soup. I think that is what it was—it was good and it was hot, and I was starving. He also left me a horse blanket that I was thankful for. I needed all the warmth I could get. I drifted off to sleep exhausted.

The next morning the two others were down below in the main part of the barn exercising. They saw that I was

TWICE SURREAL

up, and the Yank said, "Come on down. They are going to bring us some breakfast." Sure enough, the door opened and the young boy had a tray with mugs, tea, scrambled eggs, potatoes, and bread. We shared the food and ate, with little conversation. Actually, I don't remember talking to them at all. I was trying to justify in my mind how all this could have taken place in just a little over twenty-four hours. I just kept repeating to myself to say nothing except my rank, name, and serial number. That's how we were trained.

Shortly after breakfast I was summoned to the house. Three men at a table requested that I sit down. One spoke broken English; he could have been Polish, but I'm not sure. He asked to see my dog tags. Then he asked me the names of the English princesses. They asked me if I knew were the Strand Hotel was located. They then informed me that they would attempt to transfer me through the underground to Spain. I was to go back to the barn and remain inside with the others. I mentioned that I did not have shoes. They answered that they would take care of finding a pair. They asked if I wanted to give up my weapons. I said, "No", and they did not make it an issue. I went back to the barn.

About an hour later, they brought in jackets for all of us, a pair of shoes for me—too small, but shoes. They took the jackets of the others, but not mine as it was under my shirt, and burnt them in a fifty gallon metal barrel. We were then told to walk to the main road, where there would be a bus stop. We were to follow this individual and when we got on the bus to separate, and leave the bus when we saw this person leave. On departing the bus, we were to cross the street and enter the garden pub or bar, whatever they call them, and to sit at a table until another person contacted us. We were to order three beers and no more and sit there sipping until we were contacted. We were given exact change for the bus. We had money in our escape kits, but did not use it for the bus.

We followed instructions and got off the bus in Antwerp, walked across the street, and took a table. We ordered the beer; the person serving did not request money, so I assume he was connected with the underground. We were surprised to see German soldiers in the same place, boisterous and drinking. They did not pay any attention to the other patrons or to us. We were of course very nervous and trying to act like one the locals.

We were only in the beer garden a short time when a person dressed like a farmer gave us a nod and as previously instructed we followed him at a distance. One of us and then the other two followed the man through the streets for what seemed like miles. I don't know for sure. Under the circumstances, every minute seemed like an hour. We followed him into an alley and there was a truck, small like a pick-up with a homemade enclosure on the back. We were told to get in and they dropped the canvas back and the truck took off.

I know we must have driven two hours. I was constantly looking at the compass; we were still heading mostly south. It was a very rough ride; the winter had made big chuckholes and this driver never missed one. We were now four, as there was another fellow in the truck when we loaded. It was now about 3 pm. and the truck stopped. We got out and were ushered quickly into an isolated farmhouse and into a room with six cots. In the room was another person, so now we were five. We were fed vegetable soup, and bread; it was hot and good. We were told to sleep with our clothes on, as we could be moved at a moment's notice. They did not have to tell us—we were not about to remove our clothes.

On the second day we were told that we were south

of Brussels and that they hoped to move us into France the following day. About 9 or 10 pm. we were hurried out of bed and told to get into the truck. We had to be moved, as there was an alert. The Germans, they claimed, had information on this location and everyone had to evacuate, including the underground people. The truck drove off with the five of us in the back of the covered pickup. Three underground members were in the cab. We drove south and were about three or four miles away from the house when we heard and saw explosions possibly at the house we had just vacated. We assumed that either the Germans had blown it up or the French Maquis (underground) had. I will never know.

Suddenly the truck stopped. The driver or one of them came to the back and lifted up the tarp. He said in very poor English, "We have to leave the main road and head east." We, the five evaders, all looked bewildered.

I said, "Well, what does this mean?"

He replied, "It means that you are going to have to leave the truck and head south."

The Yank asked, "To where?" One of the other underground people came around to the back of the truck; his English was better.

He said, "We are going to head east, as we do not have a safe house at the moment. We will drive up this dirt road and at every quarter mile we will stop, and one of you will get out. Head south and try to make another contact. We are unable to help you further as we are being hunted now. If you are caught with us, you will be shot."

Then he said, "Stay off the roads as much as possible and travel by night as much as you can. Make your contacts late in the day. If you notice that the person appears very nervous, move away quickly, and try again.

We are sorry that this has happened. Godspeed and good luck."

I was out of the truck and I said to the others, "I'm out so the best of luck."

The truck moved off down the road. I noticed it had no taillight and I realized then that would not be prudent if you want to be inconspicuous. Boy, did I feel alone at that moment and it was so dark. My watch said it was a little after midnight, so it must have been the third day. I thought we had been driving for about two hours at maybe thirty miles per hour. Even that was being optimistic. Perhaps I was about forty to forty-five miles south of Brussels. I was unable to look at my cloth map as it was too dark and I had no light. It was getting cold and I thought I had better do something or I would freeze.

The sky was overcast which helped the temperature stay a little warmer. I left the road and ran into a square wire fence. I climbed over the fence and headed south at a slow pace. The land was flat and after crossing numerous fences and being spooked several times by cattle, I came upon a creek or narrow dike about six or seven feet wide. I looked at my watch and it said about 2:30-3:00 am. I am not sure on the time. I was disoriented because of the unexpected drop. I thought back to my training, especially the evasion training we received in England, which basically was to try to find shelter, any kind, somewhere and lay low until you had a definite plan. Okay, I thought, I would have to stay put until dawn breaks. I have to be able to see the terrain and have a plan. So I lay down and took a wakie-wakie pill, as I did not want to go to sleep. I did some push-ups and other exercises to keep warm.

About 5:30 some light appeared on the horizon and I reconnoitered. There was a farmhouse and a barn, with cattle in the field about a half mile straight ahead. Had I kept going last night I would have walked right up to it. I heard a dog barking. If I got too close the dog would alert the household. It started to rain. This is all I need, I thought. There was a haystack in the field close to the house. My thinking was, there is no shelter here, and if I can get to the haystack I will be able to stay dry and warm. Only the dog was between that haystack and me. I had to take the chance.

I took a running start and cleared the stream, gambling that I would not be seen and that the dog would be busy elsewhere. It was getting lighter and now I saw the road that we must have been on, running past the farm heading south. The haystack was on the opposite side, the west side of the road, but only about forty feet off the road. It was getting lighter. I crossed the road and dug myself into the haystack. I felt confident and the heat from the fermenting hay felt good and I did not see or hear the dog. I drifted into a stupor.

I was aroused by the sounds of voices and a dog barking. There was no mistaking the German accent. There were many of them, all talking at the same time. They were gathering at the haystack, I heard the bolt of rifles cocking. They shouted in German a word I knew meant, "Get out." At the same time I could hear the rifles with bayonets attached piercing the haystack. I had no choice but to give myself up or be stabbed with a bayonet.

I pushed out and standing there were six German soldiers, the farmer, the dog on a leash growling, the farmer's wife, and two children. I raised my hands over my head and was immediately searched. They took everything I had, the escape kit, my knife, the revolver. They argued over the weapons like children. They were all quite young, but then so was I. One of them said, "For you the war is over." The farmer looked at me and gave

72

me a kind of sorry shrug, as if to say they had no choice. I was baffled as to how anyone could have seen me enter the haystack. I know farmers get up early. I wish I had that answer. I speculated that it was the dog, but I discarded that, since he would have barked at the haystack. I can only presume that someone in the house did indeed see and notified the Germans.

The corporal of the group motioned me to walk to the truck they had parked in front of the farmhouse. This of course convinced me that they did indeed notify the Germans as the truck was in front of the house and the haystack was about 500 or more feet north just off the main road. The six soldiers were pleasant enough. They were sure I was an airman as they had looked at my dog tags. I entered the army truck and four of them sat opposite me. They had removed the bayonets from their rifles and one had a German Luger in his hand exposed, for my benefit I am sure. They chatted back and forth amongst themselves, paying very little attention to me.

We traveled a short distance and arrived at an army base of some kind. The guard at the gate was curious. Maybe never saw the enemy before as he stared at me and muttered something like "luft swine," and the others laughed. We proceeded into the compound and I was taken into a gray stone building and locked in a room with a cot, no windows, and just a single bulb in the ceiling. It was obvious that this was not a cell.

My parents received this notice from the Canadian
Government when I went missing in action. It was May
1944 and I was 21 years old.

PRISONER OF WAR

I was beginning to lose track of time, but I was thinking clearer and right then and there I remember saying out loud, "I am a prisoner now, and I can handle this for ten years. Then I will be looking back on this." I believed, and still do, that it was necessary first to establish the fact that I was indeed in enemy territory, that I would be treated as the enemy, and they would have control over my life. That I was not going to wake up back in my warm bed, but that I would have many hardships. I knew I had to keep my sense of humor and above all believe that I would make it. I have and had the ability to do this and I did. And as the picture unfolds you will read how others were unable to cope.

I was in the room for a couple of hours; a German guard opened the door and said, "Come with me." I followed him and he motioned to a chair. I sat for a few minutes and then was beckoned by a nurse to come into another room. At a desk was a German officer and he addressed me in perfect English with an Oxford accent, "Are you hurt? Do you have any wounds?" I showed him my wrist, which previously had been bandaged crudely.

He removed the bandage looked at the wound and said, "Flak or bullet?"

I replied, "Fragment, 20mm."

He said, "Oh! You were shot down then?"

I immediately realized that I had given him information that I should not have. I thought I would have to be more careful. I replied, "Stuart Hunt, Flying Officer, J28785 is my serial number, sir!" With that I saluted him.

He smiled and called for a nurse and told her to clean and dress the wound; it required three stitches. I was then taken back to the original room. They brought me food, soup and bread. I decided that I did not want the civilian jacket on anymore so I put it under the cot in hopes they would not find it when I was removed from this room.

I had hardly finished the food when the door opened, and heard what I was to hear so often, "Come." I followed the guard outside to a waiting black sedan and was told to get in the back seat; a soldier got in beside me. In the front were the driver and a man in civilian clothes. He spoke English, but not as well as the doctor. He said, "Airman, we are going to take a trip to an area where a plane has crashed. We want you to recognize the countryside where you have managed to avoid detection so skillfully. We want you to tell us where you got help and point out these places."

He used the word places and not houses. I am thinking, is this real? God, they would shoot these people on the spot. The ride lasted about two hours; we went through Brussels and Antwerp. I was trying to figure what to say and how to make it believable. It's uncanny how close we went to the actual spot where I hit the beach. I was thinking, has one of the crew been caught and told them who and what?

This had to be one of my worst nightmares; I realized that this person was Gestapo. He was trying to be light with me, saying that I would soon be in a POW camp and that they treated Canadians very well. He stopped the car and said, "Get out and look around. What looks familiar to you?"

I said, "It was dark and I don't recognize any particular spot."

"Did any of the people in this area help you?" he asked.

"No", I answered.

Then the bomb fell when he said, "How did you get the civilian jacket?"

Hell, he knew about the jacket. I recalled what they taught in training: name, rank, and serial number is all you had to give. I did this and he said, "Okay, airman, as far as I am concerned you were picked up in civilian clothes. Therefore, you are an infiltrator and will be sent to a concentration camp. Your memory will be better there." No other words were spoken.

We got back in the sedan and headed south through Antwerp and on to Brussels, where we stopped in the city, in front of this castle-like structure. It was the St. Gilles Prison; I did not know the name at the time. It was like going back to the time of the Count of Monte Cristo. I was taken inside and down a corridor lined with heavy wooden doors with big steel hinges. Each door also had a steel plate that was hinged so that the guards could flip it to one side to peer inside. They stopped at a cell and opened the door and pushed me in with a vengeance. You can imagine my surprise to find Graham Walker, our wireless operator, in this cell. There was a third person in the cell; I can't remember who it was.

TWICE SURREAL

Was this the third, fourth, or fifth day, I didn't know. Walker told me he had been hit with about twelve fragments of shrapnel when the plane was attacked by the German fighter that shot us down. The smell from his wounds was apparent. I called the guard, and said, "I want to see the doctor." The peephole opened and he said, "Wait," or something to that effect. In about five minutes I was taken to the medical office to see the doctor. I told the doctor that a prisoner in the cell had the start of gangrene in his arm and leg and needed attention. I said I was an officer and demanded that he be given attention as set forth by the Geneva Conventions.

He said, "You are the filthiest looking officer that I have ever come across, but we will have your cell mate brought to the dispensary."

I said, "Yes, I am rotten filthy, so why don't you let me have a bath?"

With that he called the guard and said, "Take him back to his cell." I saluted, he did not reply. I felt good about the outcome, however, as Walker was in bad shape. I never saw him again after that until the POW reunion in Calgary in 1985. It was at this meeting that he told me I probably saved his limbs.

Another coincidence that took place stands out. Previously I mentioned that at Wellsbourne there was a flyer by the name of Anderson. I used to come in late and he would be sleeping and I would hit him on the ass and shout, "Living in a great big way." Well, when the guards brought the food to us, they lifted the peephole cover, looked in, and then pushed the food in. This time the guard did not close the peephole and I looked through it as he came to the cell directly across from us. When he opened the door I saw Anderson and I was shocked! I shouted, "LIVING IN A GREAT BIG WAY!" He shouted back, "Marie!" I never saw him again. He was

Prisoner Of War

from Winnipeg, Manitoba.

A couple of days or maybe a day and a half passed, I don't remember. They had taken my watch so I only had the light from a barred window about ten to twelve feet above the floor, next to the ceiling. There was no way I could look out. They were feeding us slop twice a day and our waste was in a bucket. It was removed every other day, which meant it smelled; we managed to cover it with an old sack, which helped. Every day I was strengthening my mind and body to these abominable conditions. I still spent time trying mental telepathy to my mother telling her that I was okay.

About eight or nine o'clock on the second or third night the cell door opened and I was taken to a holding room. There were seven others in the room and I could see that they were airmen all in civilian clothes. I now had my battle jacket on the outside where it belonged. I wondered why I was with this group as it was obvious that I was in uniform now. My thoughts went back to the Gestapo person who had said to me that I would be treated as a spy. Four German soldiers came in; they put ankle straps and leather handcuffs on the eight of us. We then were loaded into a military truck. They also had tags with our names that they pinned to our clothing on the left shoulder. I have no idea why they did not pin it on the chest area.

In the truck with us were four guards; I was surprised that three of them did not look to be more than sixteen or seventeen. It seemed like we traveled for about thirty minutes. The truck stopped and we were ordered out. We were at a railroad station, which I guess was Brussels. We were not at the main part of the station, but further down the track, opposite a box car. The European box cars are smaller than ours. "Eight horses or forty men" was printed on the outside, usually in French, at least on the

79

ones I saw.

We were ordered in and the door was shut and locked. The interior had some straw on the floor, probably from cattle or horses as it had that smell. I had no idea where or what was going to happen to me at this point. I was also surprised when I realized that the other seven in the boxcar were not speaking English. This was a shock to me as I had thought they were allied airmen. I then realized they were perhaps underground or political prisoners. What was I doing with them?

It was morning when the train stopped. The door was pulled back and we were ordered out. It was then that I noticed that there were many other boxcars with civilians unloading. We seven, however, were moved immediately from the area. We walked about a half a mile and there was the camp. Looking inside through the wire I did not see any uniforms. We went through a wide gate and into the compound. We were told to wait outside what appeared to be an administration building. The leg wraps and handcuffs were removed. It was still very cold and my feet in those small shoes were causing me severe pain. I was taken into the building and then into an office off the main hallway. There was a German non-commissioned officer, a sergeant possibly. He looked at me with a look of astonishment.

"Luftwaffe?" he queried.

"Yes," I replied.

"Sit and wait", he ordered, and then left the room. As he did, the guard who was standing outside the office returned to guard me, I suppose. Ten or fifteen minutes passed and the sergeant, accompanied by another person, returned. The other person, not military, must have been an interpreter.

"There has been a mistake," he said. "You should not

be here. You will be transferred to another facility when arrangements can be made. We are unable to house you here, so you will be furnished with a blanket and are to sleep in the courtyard adjacent to this building."

I asked, "May I have a bath?" The answer was no.

"Where am I?" I asked.

He replied very impatiently, "No more questions, you will be told where to report for count in the morning."

He left. I was given a blanket, taken outside to a small courtyard, and told not to leave that area.

I lay down on the cobblestone. The area was sheltered on three sides and the weather was not as cold as before. I wrapped myself in the heavy blanket and drifted off. A guard with some food awakened me; from the sun it appeared to be early afternoon. I really could not see much of the camp from my location and could not figure why I was being kept in outdoor solitary. Later that afternoon a guard came by and beckoned me to follow. I followed to a large area, like a parade ground.

At the far side were gallows with five people on the platform with ropes around their necks. A German officer was announcing something to the mass of internees. Suddenly, the individuals disappeared, only the ropes straining from the weight, as seen from my position. I was immediately taken back to the courtyard. Why was I taken to see this spectacle? Perhaps it was to show what happened if you tried to escape and were recaptured. This is what I understood must have happened to the individuals on the gallows.

Later that evening, maybe even early morning, I was again roused and told that I was being moved. They only put the wrist cuffs on me and I was taken inside what I call the administration building. The guard pointed to a chair and I sat there for maybe two or three hours. Dawn was breaking and I was led out and into another truck. This one did not have a canvas drop so I was able to see out. Only one guard was with me. I could hear steam engines so knew that I was again at the railroad station. I was taken this time to a coach car and seated in the rear with the same guard opposite me as the seats were facing each other. I looked out the window and saw a sign that said Weimar. Later I learned that the infamous concentration camp Buchenwald was located at Weimar, so that is indeed where I had been. Now I understand why they did not want me roaming the camp; the less I knew the better. You can get the horrible details of this camp on the Internet.

The train I was on appeared to be a troop train, as I did not see any civilians. I asked the guard if I could use the toilet. He got up and took me to the lavatory. He stood outside. I went in and there was a sink with cold running water. I quickly took off my top and dropped my pants and performed the fastest spit bath ever. There were no towels but I did not care as the water felt good, cold as it was. I wet my hair and pushed it back, using my fingers as a comb. The guard knocked on the door and I said, "Ja, ja." I put my clothes back on over my wet skin. That was the first water on my body in days, a week maybe? As I came out the guard saw that I was wet and he said, "Good." I guess I must have smelled, as he did not seem to mind my having taken the spit bath.

The train stopped at a large city. I don't know the name, but I think it was along the Rhine River. I was taken off the train and put in a room in a building adjacent to the main station. I remained in there alone for about an hour or so. The handcuffs were taken off and the guard took me to another train that had just arrived. With a good bye wave and a slight smile he turned me over to another guard.

I was taken aboard and seated in a coach type rail car.

This time, however, I noticed about twenty or so other airmen, American and British Commonwealth types. Some were double-seated, others single-seated. Guards stood at either end of the coach as if this were an everyday occurrence. We traveled for some time and it was then that I noticed my Air Force ring was gone. My aunt Binnie had purchased it for me at Birks in Montreal. I was trying to remember when and where it was removed. I think at St. Gilles, but I am not sure. As a point of interest, Birks replaced it free of charge after they heard how it was stolen.

The train slowed down and we entered a large city. The station had been bombed and was a shambles; I heard someone say "Frankfurt" as we approached the station. It was totally destroyed; every building was wrecked. As I mentioned previously, it was only a few weeks back that we had bombed out 120,000. The destruction was awesome. We all knew that we were in for a very unpleasant welcome from the citizens of this city.

The guards told us to stay in a tight group and they would try to protect us from the angry mob. They kept us on the train for about thirty minutes hoping the mob would dissipate, but that did not happen. The guards informed us again that we must stay together and move with them or we would surely be beaten to death, and to get into the waiting trucks as quickly as possible. They had the area outside the coach clear and we assembled there, about twenty or twenty-five of us. The Germans had reinforcement troops at the station to help keep the mob back. It was a very terrifying experience.

I was frightened and who would not be. As we came into the main station lobby, we were completely surrounded by the soldiers. The crowds were throwing stones and bottles and gunfire was heard repeatedly, which might have been the Germans firing into the air to try and disperse the crowds. These people were livid with hate and literally wanted to tear us limb from limb. I had my arms over my head and was crouching low, but some stones and bottles still managed to hit my arms. We finally made it to the trucks and scurried into the covered back with three or four guards in the truck at the rear. The mob was trying to tip the trucks over as we drove off. From what I saw of the devastation that we had poured on this city I cannot blame the people for their actions. I can say unequivocally that had it not been for the protection of these German soldiers we would not have survived.

So we were now at the infamous "Transit Camp of the Luftwaffe" in Oberursel, or Dulag Luft. We were never informed in England of this camp or what to expect. We exited from the truck and were escorted into a waiting room. Then by name we were to be interviewed by the so-called "Red Cross." That is what we were told. My name was called, Officer Hunt. I was then escorted by a guard and told to sit in the chair in front of the interviewer's desk; he was dressed in civilian clothes.

This person introduced himself as a representative of the Red Cross and said that he would notify my relatives that I was a prisoner of war. He also told me that he had things like a toothbrush, bar of soap, and a comb, compliments of the RC. I remember asking him, "Does water go with the gifts?"

He gave a half-hardy laugh and went on. "First we must fill out this form so that the information can be relayed to Switzerland and then on to your relatives." So it began with my name, rank, and serial number. Okay so far, then he said, "We will need *you* to complete the questionnaire in order to complete the notification of your present status here as a POW."

Prisoner Of War

He handed me a pen and the questionnaire. I looked at it and the questions were type of plane, date of your mission, area shot down, how many in the crew, squadron location and number, name of commanding officer.

After looking it over, I handed it back and said, "Under the Geneva Conventions all that I am required to give you is name, rank, and serial number." His English broke into German and shouted at me, to scare me I'm sure, "Don't you want us to help you?"

I said, "You will help me by notifying the Red Cross of my interment with my name and rank and serial number."

With that he called the guard and I was roughly hauled to a solitary cell about four by eight feet with no window, only the proverbial bare light bulb. The only "furniture" was a two foot wide wooden cot, four legs with a wood surface and a blanket. I didn't know at the time that this was to be my home for the next few weeks. It's a mystery to me why most Germans had to imitate Hitler by screaming every time they needed to make a point.

Before we entered the building, they had deloused us for lice with a powder spray. They would put the nozzle inside your shirt, front and back and gave you a blast; our hair was gray from the powder. It was necessary, as lice were a problem.

So here I was in a German interrogation camp. The cells were wood walls and not thick; I could hear conversation through the walls on each side of me, whenever the guard had to converse with a prisoner. The building was new, a few years old, built especially for its present use. The toilet facilities were better than all my previous rentals. During the day—at night you used a small pail in the cell—when you had the need to use a toilet, you hollered for the guard. He would take you and stand outside while you did your thing. There were three washbasins and three lavatories. You were never inside with another prisoner; there was no communication allowed whatsoever. So when you had to go you had to wait until the room was empty. There was soap and a dirty towel, which may have been clean in the morning, but by evening it was black. One towel. Surprisingly, there was a comb and we did get toothbrushes that had to be left in the bathroom with your cell number on it, but no toothpaste.

It was like this for days; I was talking with the guy in the next cell using Morse code by tapping on the wall. He claimed he was a major in the U.S. Air Corps. He probably was. We battered back and forth about nothing just to pass the time. We were fed twice a day, potatoes mostly and black bread, which I learned to like. Sometimes it was sauerkraut soup. There was no breakfast type food; it was pretty much the same day in day out.

One day the prisoner next to me shouted, "Let's sing a song."

"Okay," I said. "What do you want to sing?"

He replied, "Nothing can stop the Army Air Corps."

So with a boisterous voice I burst into, "Off we go into the wild blue yonder, flying high..." The door of my cell was smashed against the wall and this guard came in with blazing eyes and his pistol in his hand screaming, "Fertig, fertig," which means stop or finish, I later learned. He pushed the handgun into my stomach so hard that I fell back on my ass on the cot. I looked at the .45 he was holding, realized that it was American, and calmly said to him, "Americana." I remember this well, because he looked at me in astonishment and said, "Ja." He then put the gun in his holster and left shaking his head. I never did the singing bit again.

One morning the door opened. The guard told me to wash. It seemed that all the guards could speak some English. He said for me to shave and gave me a razor. I had a hell of a time with this. Even though I do not have a heavy beard, it was long. The only soap was the bar soap that looked like it had been used by car mechanics. I did welcome the clean up, however, and with a few swipes here and there it felt good. I wet my hair and used the filthy comb. I was wondering what was up, but had an idea that I was going for interrogation. I was marched out of the building to another building about 300 or 400 feet away. I noticed the transit camp running parallel to this building. I saw familiar uniforms and a couple of the individuals in the compound waved to me. The compound appeared crowded with allied airmen.

I was ushered down a hall and into an office. Sitting behind a large desk was an officer in his entire splendor. His uniform was beautifully tailored; an iron cross on his chest was held there by a striped ribbon around his neck. He was very striking indeed, with his leather boots and riding type britches, the office immaculate, maps on the walls, floors spotless. If they were trying to impress me, I was impressed. I felt so unkempt at that moment. I saluted and he returned the courtesy.

"Well, Flying Officer Hunt," he said in perfect Oxford English. "I hope you have been treated well."

"As well as can be expected," I replied.

He then went on about how well the German POWs were treated in Canada and other small talk. He mentioned that perhaps I would like to take a walk for some exercise as I had been locked up for a time. He did not wait for an answer, but opened the door and proceeded to walk with me out of the building, with the guard following. We walked around the area and he discussed how wrong it was that we should be fighting each other when the enemy was the Russians. He was convinced, he said, that we would all have to deal with this problem, meaning the Russians. It was very confusing to me, to be walking around like this, with the small talk. What was the bottom line?

We got back to the office and I remember this conversation like it was yesterday. He said, "Officer Hunt, we do not need information from you. We have all that. We have the names of your crew," and he named them. "We know your squadron and location, we even know the name of your commanding officer. What we need from you is confirmation. It is not necessary for you to give me any other intelligence." He used that word, "intelligence".

I replied, "Sir, I am only required to give you my name, rank, and serial number, which you have." I reminded him that he was an officer and knew the rules of the Geneva Convention.

He left it there and said to me, "What do you think of our German Luftwaffe?"

"They are no f---ing good," I answered.

His reaction to this remark was like a bomb explosion. He jumped out of his leather chair, and with two leaps was at the door of the office, grabbing the guard and in German shouting to get this prisoner back to solitary. He just about scared me to death with the way he came out of his leather swivel chair. He was really ticked, and I was not treated kindly on the way back to my hovel. The guard repeatedly hit me on the back with his rifle; I was waiting to be hit on the head, but fortunately that did not happen. I was glad to get back to my cell, as I was bruised and hurting.

Well, Stuart, how stupid can you be, I thought. Just when things were looking better you have to say something so stupid to a Luftwaffe officer. Now will I ever get out of here? God! How stupid! I was in agony thinking that with all my training that I would not respect his military branch. Here was an officer who seemed to be treating me equally and with respect, regardless of his motives. I spend the rest of that day and night, and all the days and nights that followed, despising myself for creating my own dilemma.

New prisoners would come and go, but I was still in that box. It was weeks. Then one morning the guard came and said, "Come. You will wash and shave." So I knew that I was to reappear again, with the same officer. I saluted. He returned the salute.

"So, Flying Officer Hunt, how is your stay?" he asked. I replied that I had had better accommodations.

"Well," he said, "We really do not need any more information from you so I am going to send you to the transit compound. There you will be able to get a hot shower and fresh clothes and clean up the ones you have."

"Thank you, sir," I responded.

"Yes," he said. "I noticed how difficult it is for you to walk in those shoes you have. French, aren't they?"

"I am not sure, sir. I found them in a barn I took shelter in." He looked at me knowing I was lying.

He then said, "What part of Canada are you from?"

I said, "Winnipeg."

"How interesting," he said. "We have an officer here whose wife is from Winnipeg, would you like to talk to her?" He dialed the phone and then put it down saying there was no answer. I did not know where this was going. "I will mention to her that I had talked to a fellow Winnipegian. What street did you say you lived on?" he asked.

"Dominion Street," I replied.

With that he called the guard and gave instructions to take me to the transit compound. I saluted and left.

Why I said I lived in Manitoba just came out of the blue. Every city in Canada has a Dominion Street. I entered the transit and then was interrogated by our own camp intelligence officers. This was done to determine that you were indeed an allied military person and not a German plant.

So I had a "hot" shower. Little did I realize that this would be the last hot shower I would have until the end of the war. You were only allowed one hot shower a week in this camp due to fuel shortage as the water was heated using coal. I got clean undergarments and a pair of larger boots, which still did not fit properly, being a shade small. They were able to clean my battle uniform up a little. It looked better, but a long way from acceptable in military circles.

I did not see any of our crew in the compound, but one of them must have been through here. How else would they have known our names, station, and type of plane? As it turned out I never found out and it is just as well.

The following day I was again summoned to the office of the interrogator. They had a mechanical drawing of the Halifax Mark III pinned on the wall. Penciled in the drawing was the under gunner's turret. In the office were two other officers. I was introduced and all spoke English well.

"Flying Officer Hunt," the interrogator explained, "these men are engineers and are interested in the new configuration shown here on the underside of your Halifax. Due to the damage, we were unable to determine the field of fire. We did notice that the weapon was a single 50 caliber. The reason for your being here is to draw lines on this chart showing the approximate field of fire."

I was stunned that they would even know the plane was mine and to have such details. The truth of the matter was that I did not know the answer, and I told them so. I explained that I had never been in the under turret, as this plane was new to me. Glances went back and forth and I was told to go back to the compound.

The next day we boarded a train and were transferred to the fastest growing prisoner of war camp in the world, Stalag Luft III. We were marched to the camp from the rail station, stopping for delousing and to have our pictures taken. I was issued a pot metal dog tag, tied around my neck with a shoelace. This was my new name, number 5120. I still have it. I had it gold plated and it always starts conversation at the POW reunions.

TWICE SURREAL

This is a photograph of St. Gilles as it looks today.

I was imprisoned in Saint Gilles located in Brussels Belgium during the first weeks of my capture. I think my stay was about a week or so.

Prisoner Of War

This is a photograph of Buchenwald concentration camp as it looks today.

After my capture, I was here for a short stay - approximately for 36 hours. I was then transferred to an interrogation camp near Hamburg before I was transferred to Stalag Luft III.

The reason I was sent here was partly due to the civilian clothes that I was wearing at the time of my capture.

STALAG LUFT III

―――――――――――――――――――――

Stalag Luft III had five compounds of allied airmen who had been shot down or otherwise captured by the Germans. This was a measure of the intensity of the bombing offensive against Germany. I was placed in the north camp, the home of the "Great Escape" of movie fame. Of the seventy-two who attempted to escape, three eventually reached England and freedom. Tragically, fifty of them were murdered in cold blood after their recapture, on direct orders from Hitler. The entire prison population fell into a state of despair and anger after hearing of this terrible act carried out by the Germans.

The ashes of these brave men were returned in urns by the Germans. The prisoners built a stone memorial that stands today in their honor. The urns were interred in this memorial. It is my understanding that a society in Germany takes care of the upkeep.

My life started the same as the last stop, interrogation by our own and then assigned a room. Due to the crowded conditions, rooms that were designed for four now had eight. The room was sixteen by sixteen feet, and if that sounds big, it was not. My first room assignment was in block 107. Two of the eight were shot down in early 1940, two in 1943, and the rest of us early 1944. Stalag Luft was a POW camp for officers of the various allied air forces and I believe there were approximately 9,000 to 10,000 prisoners in the five compounds. We had no contact with the other camps. In the camp we had a variety of allied airmen, including Americans, Polish, and French. You name it, we had some. Stalag Luft III was in Sagan, a part of Poland taken over by the Germans.

The camp was organized internally with strict rules, administered by military rank. In addition to strict military behavior, we were controlled as to what we could or could not do, including escape attempts. If you had a plan you would have to submit it to the head of the X organization. If the plan was feasible and proved viable, then it might be approved. Also, over the years this organization had bribed many guards, thereby forcing them to bring in the needed things that would be required, and crystal radio to listen to the BBC radio broadcast. All major escape plans were also approved or disapproved by code on the BBC radio. How the codes were transmitted to us remains a mystery to me, as I was never privy to that information.

Every individual was assigned some form of duty. The duties were too numerous to mention. One example was keeping tally on what German goons were in the camp. The point is that we knew at all times who, where, and what was going on in the camp. Why did we call the guards goons and gophers? "Goons" were so named after Swee'pea's monstrous babysitter in the Popeye comic strip; "gophers" was used because they were always poking in the ground looking for tunnels.

In July 1944, we were given a Red Cross parcel, which

included long underwear, socks, and a bath towel. The package also contained a pullover, a blanket, gloves, a cap, shaving soap and brush, a razor with five blades, a comb, a toothbrush and tin of tooth-powder, and few other odds and ends. It was like Christmas. We cherished this handout.

We also got the occasional Red Cross food parcel. It was not that these were scarce. The problem was that the shipping those to the camps required truck or train to transport, which were being shot up by our own fighters. We would be told that a shipment was coming in, only to be told the shipment had been destroyed. However, the Red Cross parcels kept us alive, even though they were infrequent.

The German Luftwaffe ran the camp and so there was a relationship. After the Great Escape, however, they were replaced, much to our sorrow. The German SS took over and the relationship changed drastically. You see, the German high command was so embarrassed with the escape that drastic measures were taken, security more severe, additional guards with fierce dogs patrolled the camp day and night. Blocks were searched for no apparent reason and personal belongings were sometimes destroyed. We would be called out in the middle of the night for an appell, the head count or roll call made infamous by the Germans in the concentration camps. We were often made to stand for hours if the count was not right, and even if it was right. Our senior officer complained bitterly to no avail. So we beefed up our own security and still continued with new tunnels.

The camp was enclosed by two fences of barbed wire separated by about eight feet with barbed wire in between. There was a clearing of twenty feet inside the main fence and then a single warning wire a foot off the ground. If you stepped over this wire you would be shot.

Unfortunately, as many as nine or ten prisoners were shot either trying to escape, or perhaps they just went stir crazy and rushed the fence.

Our main concern was to stay in shape. There were no fat prisoners as I remember, and ribs were the dress of the day as we exercised. We only wore our under shorts in the summer, it was warm.

We constructed a set of parallel bars and a high bar. I was doing well on the bars with the help of a former Olympic contender who was a prisoner. Time was also spent reading. I read about forty books that had been accumulated over five years from parcels sent to prisoners and furnished by the Red Cross. We also had playing cards and we played bridge. I never played again after that.

Because we were officers, the Germans did not put us to work. So to keep our minds alert we dug tunnels and employed other means of escape, although the chance of making it back to England was very unlikely. In some of the care parcels sent, all sorts of escape aids were concealed, some in the handles of ping pong paddles. There were things like dye for making German uniforms, money, and pens with different shades of ink. Aids would be inside of shaving soap, all very ingenious methods of sending needed articles to us.

We were marched out of the camp in small groups for delousing every month. Here's an example of how clever some of the prisoners were. They made a German uniform out of a blanket, boots out of cardboard and old leather flying jackets. A rifle was made of wood. The prisoner who wanted the uniform made put it on and marched a group of our prisoners to the gate, claiming he was taking them for delousing. The guard opened the gate and they marched out. They were down the road before the guard realized that he did not recognize this guard and they were recaptured. Prisoners, hiding under the trash in a wagon and attempting to pass through the camp gates, tried numerous methods. This usually proved fruitless.

At night we would play Russian roulette with the camp searchlights and the roving guards with dogs. In the center on the camp was a building that the Germans used to store some food and coal blocks. The trick was to avoid being caught as you climbed through a window and in a sack stole as many blocks of coal as you could and anything that was edible. We would have to beat the lights from the towers by running into the shadows of the block buildings and time the swinging of the searchlights. As the doors were locked each night we would have to make sure that the window could be unlocked from the inside the room, as this was our only exit. Then one of us—we rotated—would have to slip out and go for it. The dogs were our greatest fear and timing was the secret of success. We would have to know how many guards and dogs were in the camp; it was a challenge. We never got caught; if we had it would have been thirty days in the cooler.

Life in the camp really boiled down to how to survive, survive, and survive. We were buoyed by the news of "D-Day", June 6, 1944 . Our hopes of liberation soared. We would be out in a week was the word. Of course, that did not happen and it was a year later before we enjoyed freedom again.

As the summer wore on the action in the skies increased and we would be privy to air battles overhead. We would lie down on the ground and watch as the fighters would attack the B-17s. We would shout for joy when a German fighter was smoking and spiraling down. Mostly, however, it was our bombers being ripped apart, some exploding in midair, others trailing smoke. We would count the parachutes as the crews exited from the crippled planes. Very seldom did we see a full crew exit; in fact, I can't recall one. As the war moved into the fall months we saw more fighter vs. fighter activity. We were also getting rumbles from the eastern front. The Russians were moving closer to our camp.

Winter came on us with a bang, real cold. The shower room had no hot water, which was passable in the summer. In the winter it was unbearable. As you stood naked the heat of your breath showed like smoke from an automobile exhaust. You could not stand under the water when it was running. You just dashed through it, caught your breath, soaped a little and ran back under it. Then you ran bare ass back to the block to try and warm up. Usually the pipes were frozen and the Germans would have to come in and blow torch the pipes to thaw them out. You had to leave some water running or the pipes would freeze. The shower floor was always frozen, sometimes with ice a half inch thick until we were able to break it up and dispose of it. Needless to say very few showers were taken.

The war had bogged down on the western front, but the Russians were getting close to us. We did not want to be liberated by the Russians, as reports were not encouraging about the way prisoners were treated. The fact is that many allied prisoners who were liberated by the Russians were never heard from again.

Food parcels were scarce as the year 1944 was coming to a close. The allied air forces had complete control of the air and anything that moved was destroyed or damaged. The Germans claimed that in Denmark there were thousands of Red Cross parcels that they were unable to transport. The Germans themselves were in a food shortage. Christmas and the new year passed and we moved into the year 1945.

Stalag Luft III

The following account is the worse experience my body and mind has ever been subjected to.

The approximate strength at Stalag Luft III was 10,000 Officers and other ranks, over 90% being officers. I am only going to report on my experiences and the approximate 2,000 in the group of the North Compound.

Being a camp for air force prisoners only, Stalag Luft III included some of the oldest POWs in Germany. A few were in their sixth year of captivity and a high proportion had been prisoners for three or more years.

Since June 1944 communication on the continent of Europe had been so interrupted that the last four months of that year all prisoners at Sagan (now Zagan, Poland) had received only half parcels per week instead of the prescribed whole. Our diet as analyzed by a nutrition expert was 1,000 calories per day per head below normal requirements and well below a healthy standard. This included German rations. One week prior to the evacuation the issue of a full parcel was re-commenced. The physical standard was therefore below normal, a point that must be fully considered in relation to the long and arduous marches that ensued.

The mental health of prisoners had been affected with measures taken by the Germans as a result of the escape of the seventy-six officers from our camp. Fifty of the officers were summarily shot on re-capture, as I noted previously. The effect of this atrocity on our spirits was depressing. This was accentuated by other reprisals taken, which included restriction of parole walks and total suspension of inter-compound communication.

By January 19, 1945, the Russians had advanced to within striking distance of Breslau and Posen. It was then that a move of the prisoners from Sagan became a possibility. Our CO made inquiries to the

101

Kommandantur, and the reply was that no move was contemplated. The Germans were confident that they would hold at the River Oder. On the 20th, the Russians reached the Oder and crossed it south of Breslau. Still the camp kommandant reiterated that a move would not be necessary, but gave a qualified consent that backpacks could be made. This was Monday the 22nd of January. We wanted to dig slip trenches for protection should the camp come within the battle area. The answer was no.

During the week of the 21st to the 27th of January the Russians continued their advance up the Oder, North of Breslau, and artillery fire could be heard. We heard news that British camps near Breslau were on the move westwards. We were not being threatened, and we became a center for refugees.

Meanwhile we were all preparing for a march either under German or Russian auspices. We were given advice as to what to carry and how much weight. The suggestion was between twenty and forty pounds. We were concerned about what food and clothing to take; boots were overhauled. This was a very weak point in my case, as I could not put extra socks on as the boots were too small. It is interesting that the circuit around the camp became crowded throughout the day with people training for marching. Up to the evening of the 27th of January no change in the attitude of the German camp authorities occurred. We asked for permission to make sleds to carry extra food and supplies, but it was denied. Several built sleds and they were confiscated.

We learned that the Germans had been issued two days' rations. There were other orders from the high command regarding sick prisoners. Those with minor ailments were to march and the more seriously ill were to stay in the camp. We therefore believed the Kommandantur had indeed received orders for a move. These orders were not conveyed to us, which added to the subsequent confusion.

We did not know when the exact order was given, but it must have been between 1800 and 1900 hours on Saturday, January 27th. It was at this time that the kommandant received the order from Berlin that the camp at Sagan was to march at once. Many of the German administration staff were in town and it took time to round them up. This created a problem as the information was given to the camps at different times. We were told at 2000 hours with a deadline of 2100 hours as the zero hour. Because liberation by the Russians seemed imminent, our camp commander told us to stay put—that we would not go on the march. The Germans, however, changed our minds by firing their machine guns down the halls of the blocks. This has a way of changing your mind. No rations were issued, but we were allowed to take one Red Cross parcel each.

It was then that permission was granted to make sleds as long as they did not hold up the march. Several hundred sleds were made from the slats in the bunks. I did not make a sled; I had a backpack of sorts. Our camp was ready to march as instructed. I understand that other camps had delays.

The compounds were left in a state of chaos. There was no time to collect all our belongings. I was told that in all the camps at least 23,000 Red Cross food parcels were left behind intact. Owing to the indecision over sleds and the fact we could only take what we could carry, much of the food from the parcels later issued for the march had to be jettisoned, involving additional waste. You can imagine how much personal property had accumulated by prisoners over a six-year span. All this had to be left. A lot of property belonged to the Red Cross. It was estimated that 250,000 pounds sterling (one million U.S. dollars) worth of supplies in all six camps was left to German poachers. At least one million cigarettes were left in our camp, the north compound. I carried as many packs as I had room for, as cigarettes were valuable trading items.

This photograph shows an example of the three bunk bed arrangement in a POW room. In our room at Stalag Luft III North Compound, we had twin bunks.

Albert Wallace was one of my roommates at Stalag Luft
III. We have remained close friends to this day.

Stalag Luft III

STALAG LUFT III – TUNNEL MARTYRS

On March 24, 1944, the single largest escape during World War II of Prisoners of War took place from the North Compound of Stalag Luft III, Sagan, Germany.

Under cover of a moonless night, 76 Allied Airforce POWs broke out from a tunnel 348 feet in length, situated 30 feet underground, in their determined bid for freedom.

The heroic attempts of the escapees ended in tragedy when 50 of the participants were murdered on orders from Adolph Hitler in direct contravention to the Geneva Agreement which prohibited such atrocities. Three escapees made it to Britain, and freedom, defying an exhaustive manhunt by German military and civilian forces. The rest were returned to various prisons and concentration camps.

Artist Bill Holder depicts the sequence of events of this escape attempt in the above painting titled **"Stalag Luft III Tunnel Martyrs."** We see an ill-fated Lancaster bomber in trouble with flack and caught in searchlights, the capture of the airmen, and the layout of the wire-enclosed prison campsite in which they were held.

Then came the plan for an escape tunnel. Here are men stationed as lookouts (one at the window, another ready to remove the stove, which covered the entrance to the tunnel being dug), the dangerous, tedious and difficult excavation work in the confined final escape tunnel dubbed "Harry." The contrast of the gold-coloured sand on the snow emphasizes the difficulty of dispersing the excavated sand undetected by the guards.

Finally, we see the daring departure by night. The tunnel unfortunately came up short of the woods; and required a hastily arranged system to guide the escapees from the mouth of the tunnel into the woods. Then, the appalling murders of the officers by the Gestapo, and the monument constructed to honour the gallant Tunnel Martyrs. Surrounding this memorial picture are the German POW Identity Photographs of the murdered airmen.

This painting, wherever it is shown, will serve as a tribute to the sacrifice of the gallant 50 – a sacrifice never to be forgotten.

This is a copy of a print I own painted by Bill Holder. The picture is a graphic detail of the "The Great Escape".

The photos surrounding the painting are the 50 airmen who were murdered on orders from Hitler.

107

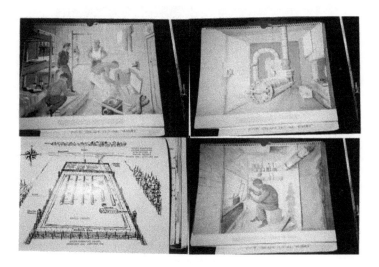

These paintings depict the Great Escape from Stalag Luft III.

Picture 1 (top left) - Room 104 where the entrance to the tunnel started.

Picture 2 (bottom left) – This is a map of the North Compound.

Picture 3 (top right) - The bellows that were built from Kim powdered milk containers to pump air into the tunnel.

Picture 4 (bottom right) - Workroom 30 feet below the surface at the entrance to tunnel.

Picture 1 (top left) – This picture shows the start of the tunnel from room 104 to the end, which was some 335 feet to the outside of the compound wire. The tunnel was supposed to end in the woods outside the fence, but it fell short.

Picture 2 (top right) -   This picture shows the working area below the entrance to the tunnel.

Picture 3 (bottom left) – This is a picture of the memorial that was built by the prisoners for the fifty airmen shot on orders from Hitler.

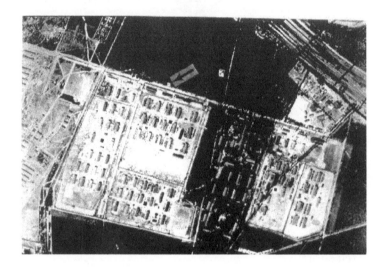

Aerial view of the prison camp, Stalag Luft III.

THE FORCED MARCH

A t 0100 hours on the morning of Sunday, the 28th of January, the north camp began to leave. At 0315 hours the last man cleared the camp. I left in the middle at about 0200 hours. (The various camps went in different directions; e.g., the American compound was moved south to Nuremberg.)

The weather was a bitter enemy. It began with six inches of snow on the ground, and for the first five days was very cold, at times intensely so. There were several severe snowstorms that added to the difficulties by soaking both kit and clothing, so that they froze. I remember that on the fifth night we had a sudden thaw. From then on it both rained and snowed frequently, making conditions underfoot sodden. To make matters worse there was a no organization on the part of the Germans.

I mentioned we were given a Red Cross food parcel in the German annex as we left the camp. Most of this as mentioned previously was discarded the first mile as a result of overloading caused by the issue, as we were unable to incorporate the stuff into our packs. So the German civilians had a field day.

The weather took its toll early. Some our comrades were showing the effects of the weather and poor physical condition. If you fell out you would die of exposure. It was at once evident that the Germans had made no provisions to handle this situation. There was no vehicle or horse drawn wagon to help the fallen. It was left to us; we would take turns helping the weak and sick by literally carrying the individual. This, of course, weakened the helpers. The guards themselves were in bad condition—the weather was so severe. For the most part they marched in groups making little attempt to patrol the column. By the second day, many guards were unfit for duty and one so severely frostbitten that our understanding was that he would have to have both legs amputated.

The column stretched on for miles, completely disorganized. The eight from our room stayed together, helping each other. I remember as I walked this god-forsaken countryside thinking about things in my childhood that was associated with cold and winter. How when I played hockey and my feet would be frozen and how it hurt while they thawed out. How cold I would get delivering papers on a bike, riding four to six miles in freezing weather. I did not know how long this would go on, but I said to Al Wallace, "I am not going to die in this hell hole." He gave a brief laugh and said, "We could use a little hell right now to warm us up." That was about all the humor we could muster.

Later I learned that there were two horse drawn wagons that carried German kit and some rations in the rear of the column. The Germans provided little for stragglers or the sick. Someone told me that there was a small ambulance but I never saw one.

The Forced March

Basically the organization of the march was left to the prisoners; the German officer in charge, a major, had no experience in handling a march of 2,000 men in one column, without intervals between sections. The column was constantly expanding and contracting. This caused short halts but no actual rest periods.

The first halt was supposed to be Halbau, a distance of seventeen kilometers from Sagan; we had no information about the route. Again, I want to emphasize the bitter cold temperature, well below zero, and with the wind I have no idea what the wind-chill would have been. I saw men made to abandon their sleds and kits at gunpoint if they could not keep up, and civilians were there to pick up the spoils. I don't remember the exact time we reached Halbau. I know it got increasingly colder, with intermittent snow and darkness, which caused the guards as much difficulty as the prisoners. It was only our fierce determination that brought us through.

When we reached Halbau, no provision had been made for the issue of rations or water by the German authorities. We halted for one hour. The civilians with rare exception were friendly and a few got some hot water. Our group was not that lucky. Many of the guards prevented the civilians from giving us anything, water included. I do not remember the German military authority providing us with water. So we would have to eat snow for liquid, which was hard to do as the clean snow would be in the fields and you were not allowed to leave the road. I recall a guard knocked a pot of water from a woman's hands as she was attempting to give water. In many cases these guards held the prisoners back and took the food and water for themselves. If you were able to make a contact then you could barter with cigarettes for some food. I never got the chance; some of the more fluent in German did, however.

TWICE SURREAL

At Halbau the column was informed that it was to billet for the night at Freiwaldan, eleven kilometers further on. This village was reached about noon. We were very tired, and without adequate meals or rest stops. There was little or no attempt to find accommodations and the two barns allotted were totally inadequate. We waited for an hour exhausted and half-frozen when we were told to find our own arrangements. The senior British officer pointed out in no uncertain terms to Major Rostek the condition of the prisoners, and the need for organized shelter. The Major promised, but nothing was done. There was an objection to the prisoners being there, made either on the part of civilian or military authorities in the town that led to the decision by the Germans that the march had to be resumed.

We had already marched twenty-eight kilometers. With frequent stationary periods, it was impossible to take off packs because of lack of information about the duration of the halts. These occurred in frequent snowstorms and a steadily decreasing temperature. Again it was bitterly cold. Clothes and packs were soaked, and the absence of bread and, for most of us, any warm food, was beginning to tell. We marched to a small village named Leipp about six kilometers further on. The column was in very grim condition. We were all feeling the weight of our packs, and we were marching now with backs slightly bent, stopping every now and then to give the pack a lift on the shoulder or bending double to give the muscles a rest. For many of us it was all we could do to keep going.

I know that for me I became aware of the great weight on my feet. Everything seemed to become blurred at times; the guards became indistinguishable from the prisoners. There was frequent presence of refugees on the road, and the knowledge that the march of British prisoners was part of gigantic retreat of armies and people westward. You could make comparison with Napoleon's retreat from Moscow. Almost incessantly, far away to the north was the sound of artillery and weapon fire. Now we were hoping the Russians would come to the rescue. The column stretched for more than three miles, and looked more like a string of refugees than a military movement. Only the preponderance of air force blue jackets and sweaters gave some sort of clue to the real nature of the company.

The German major had sent an NCO forward to check the accommodations at Leippa and reported that only one barn was available for billeting. There was no further action to obtain additional refuge for the prisoners. The barn would only accommodate 600 and we were 2,000. When we reached Leippa, I was in the group that was put in the barn, where not 600 but 700 were crowded in. The rest of the column stood an additional 4 hours, which was the severest experience on the march. We had covered thirty-four kilometers and had been on the move for about eighteen hours, without any organization or hot meals. Darkness fell and it was one of the coldest nights of the year, a further heavy fall of snow occurring about midnight. Our clothes and boots were covered with ice due to early slush. It was impossible to obtain a drink and the preparation of even cold food was virtually impossible, owing to darkness and the numbness of our hands.

Major Rostek, without whose authority no German would act, could not be found. The guards in charge paid no attention to the request that we move forward in the only direction where additional billets may be found. Eventually Major Rostek was located. The senior British officer offered "parole" that no prisoner would escape during the night providing everybody could find shelter. (According to Wikipedia, the US Department of Defense defines parole agreements as promises given the captor by a POW to fulfill stated conditions, such as not to bear arms or not to escape, in consideration for special privileges, such as release from captivity or lessened restraint.) This was accepted, and eventually more barns were found. Many of our officers were now suffering from frostbite and vomiting. No medical assistance was forthcoming from the Germans. Our own medical staff did what they could but was severely handicapped because of lack of equipment.

Meanwhile, back at the original barn with the 700 crowded in where I was billeted the conditions were deplorable. Huge rats also occupied the premises. I had never seen rats that large before or since. We were so crowded that we did benefit from the heat generated from each other; we lay down in the "S" position not only by necessity, but also for warmth. But it was bitterly cold. Problems like the need to urinate created problems and many being unable to move in the darkness just urinated in their clothes. Others had dysentery and the stench was unbearable. An example of our conditions would be like sardines in a can. That night is so very vivid in my mind. We were in the lowest human condition, and little did I realize that it was going to get worse.

The issue of a third of a loaf of bread per man was attempted, but few prisoners obtained this food owing to the disorganization, the lack of knowledge of the locations of the billets, and darkness. Little water could be obtained. We were cautioned against eating the snow, as this was the cause of dysentery.

I know for a fact that on the road several officers collapsed and were found lying in a ditch by a search party organized by the prisoners themselves. No guards were present, and had no search been made, these men would have died of hypothermia.

The march was resumed at 0800 hours on Monday,

the 29th of January. It was still freezing hard. Owing to the presumed inefficiency of the guards, companies received very little notice of the start and consequently the rest of the column was kept waiting on the road. Moving was better than standing. A further long delay arose from an ineffectual attempt on the part of the Germans to make a count of the prisoners. The fact that the full complement was present, minus the ones too sick to continue, was due entirely to the organization of the prisoners themselves.

At about 1130 hours the town of Priebus was reached, and a halt of half-hour was granted, which gave us a little time to eat what we had left of the Red Cross parcel. I am not sure but I believe we left a few more prisoners here due to illness, under German scrutiny.

Muskau was reached about 1800 hours and for the first time there was evidence of organization on the part of the German military. This was due I am sure to the efforts of the senior British officer after having in mind the condition of the billeting the previous night. Major Rostek informed him that he could not guarantee accommodations, as it was necessary to keep the prisoners in a body. There were too few guards to allow dispersal. In a body they would be required to spend the night "as best they might." The major had consented, however, to arrange for accommodations providing a "parole" was given that prisoners would not escape whilst in billets. In view of our condition and the almost certain severe injury or perhaps loss of life, should we not have shelter, the senior officer gave the parole required. This parole was to stay in effect until the day following our arrival at Muskau.

Billets in Muskau were provided in a cinema (300), a glass factory (600), a stable (150), a laundry (80), a pottery works (100), and a French POW camp (300). All the billets were crowded. I was in the glass factory.

TWICE SURREAL

It was in the glass factory that I started to vomit and the dysentery started. We were able to get a little fire going on the concrete floor and heated up some of the remnants of the food parcel. It must have been the water that started me into dysentery. Many experienced the vomiting and I do not know what caused it. Although we were in shelter, there was no heat and many of the windows of the factory had been broken. We managed to stay somewhat comfortable, but I was really sick. My roommates wanted me to stay behind, but I refused vigorously, saying, "I am not staying here to be picked up by the Russians; I will die walking first."

After much pleading I convinced them not to report me. Many prisoners were left in Muskau for medical attention, how they fared I do not know.

We were informed that our stay would only be twenty-four hours, but it was not until 2300 hours on Thursday, the 1st of February that we left, around 11 p.m. In the meantime, 1500 Red Cross food parcels from Sagan were partially issued as well as one-third a loaf of bread per man. Again owing to bad German administration, not everyone received a parcel or bread. In our group, I think we got two parcels for the eight of us and no bread.

Reflecting back a moment, I recall on the afternoon of Wednesday, January 31st, 500 or more American officers and men of the USAAF who were in our camp at Sagan left us to join a column from an American camp. The same evening about 1,050 British officers and other ranks from the east compound reached Muskau.

On the afternoon of February 1st, the Germans ordered our camp, which was the north compound, along with 600 from east compound, to march that night for Spremberg. We were to board the train in cattle cars. No marching rations were issued. The column consisting of about 1,900 officers and men moved from the town in complete darkness at about 2300 hours. We left fifty-seven members from the north compound behind as too sick to march. I was too sick to march as well, but refused to stay behind. In the days to follow, I questioned my decision many times.

We had a sudden thaw the previous evening and most of the sleds were abandoned as the snow melted on the road. Even in the open country it had thawed too hard, leaving slush and more wet boots. From the effects of the previous marches, I saw more than one officer had frostbite so badly that they were unable to wear their boots and finished the march in socks. The darkness, the hilly nature of the county, and the continued failure of the Germans to exercise normal march discipline made this the most difficult stage of the journey. For me it was a nightmare having to squat and defecate along side of the road, and then try to catch up with our group. It was cold; I was in deep sweats and dehydrated.

The guards, many of whom were loudly complaining, soon abandoned any serious attempt to patrol and straggled along with the prisoners. The prisoners themselves marched in companies, with little conversation above the sound of muffled footsteps. Many sick dropped behind; I was almost ready to give it up. Only the hardiest had any spring left in their stride by the time the night was through. When halts where ordered many had to be dragged to their feet to go on. Guards would fire shots close to men who lagged.

The column reached a village named Graustein, seven kilometers from Spremberg, at 600 hours on the 2nd of February. We halted here until about 1100 hours. We were provided barns to stay in. The farmer supplied us with hot water in the barn we were in, so we did have a hot drink, the first since Jan 27th.

TWICE SURREAL

We reached Spremberg at approximately 1500 hours and we were held in what was stated to be a reserve. By 1130 hours we were on the move again. My dysentery had not let up and I was still vomiting intermittently. As we approached Spremberg, you could notice a stiffening of the guards; for the first time patrolling became efficient. For example, one of our officers was walking on the side of the road to avoid the slush and water and was shouted at by a guard. When he stopped to try and understand what was being said, he was struck with the butt end of a rifle. Civilians were prevented from giving prisoners water. I recall that one woman was attempting to give us hot coffee, only to be told by the guard to give it to the refugees. The woman burst into tears and said her husband was a prisoner in British hands and being well treated and she wished to do something in return. The guard knocked coffee from her hand, smashing the ceramic pot.

At Spremberg we were held at the depot of the 8th Panzer Division. Soup was issued to everyone within a half an hour and hot water provided. At 1600 hours the order was to march again and at 1630 hours the column left for the station, about three kilometers away. Those prisoners unable to continue remained at the depot. The number was thought to be five. I personally was in very critical condition and again my roommates encouraged me to remain. I said, "No."

Our destination was now made known for the first time, Milag und Marlag Nord camp, near Tarmstedt and about thirty kilometers from Bremen. The train ride was to be from Spremberg to Tramstadt.

On our arrival at the Spremberg railroad station, prisoners were allotted to cattle trucks—boxcars in Europe are called cattle trucks and are much smaller that our boxcars. These were the only means of conveyance for the journey of at least 300 miles. Even at the scheduled figure of forty men per truck there were too few available. In one small truck designated to hold twenty-five held forty; as many as seventy were assigned to trucks without windows. The trucks were filthy; in ours there was manure as well as human excreta, which had to be cleared away. It was impossible to lie down full length; the only possible way to sleep was in a sitting position or lying on one side wedged between neighbors and unable to alter position. These conditions were to cover two nights and two days.

Before the train left, a ration of two-thirds loaf of bread per man was issued to the British rations officer. This was distributed I believe; we also got a Red Cross food parcel that had been brought from Sagan. I know I used, with others, a lot of the boxes for our dysentery problem. Just to get into a squatting position in such crowded conditions required co-operating help from the other prisoners. The stench was vile.

According to Major Rostek, arrangements had been made to water the train at Falkenberg, which was reached at 1300 hours on the 3rd of February. The guards left the train for water but were sent back by railroad authorities, and the train went on without water. Then it was our understanding that a railway food kitchen would draw up alongside the train at Halle, but when the train reached that place at about 2130 hours, a hospital train from the east had arrived and the food was given to them. Once again the railroad authorities intervened and we moved on after a half-hour halt. Only a few cans of water were provided. At about 0730 hours on the 4th of February, the train stopped on the outskirts of Hannover. It was here that the major gave the order that water for the prisoners was to be supplied from the neighboring houses and that the train was not to move until he gave the order. This would be the first issue of water since leaving Spremberg a period of 36 hours.

As a result we were subjected to added discomfort owing to thirst and of course were prevented from relieving nature. I was now very ill and was unable to get to my feet without help. My comrades pushed others back to allow me room to lie down. I felt like I was suffocating. There were small barred windows on each side of the truck (box car); that was the only air. It was no place to be if you were claustrophobic. There was no lighting of course so it was pitch black at night and almost as dark during the day.

The Forced March

Road from Sagan: This is the route that 12,000 POWs (including myself) took when forced to evacuate the German POW camp, Stalag Luft III, near Sagan, Poland, on the night of January 27, 1945.

We were marched west for 52 miles to Spremberg, Germany into the teeth of a blizzard.

The line stretching nearly 20 miles long. At that point we were then crammed in boxcars and transported to various camps.

TWICE SURREAL

journeys to transit camps in various parts of Germany.
Those present remembered the goods sidings, opposite
the main platform, where they had boarded the train.

Here the Long March had ended.

This is a current photo of the Spremberg Railway station.

At the end of the first march, we boarded boxcars at this station and move to Tarmstedt. On the sides of the boxcars was stated "eight horses or forty persons". This style of boxcars were smaller than you see in the U.S.

ANOTHER CAMP AND MARCH

The train arrived at Tarmstedt at about 1700 hours on Sunday the 4th of February. The doors opened and we were told to stay until ordered to detrain. Our group, still together, was discussing what and how I could make the march to the camp. I was still vomiting and the dysentery had drained me of all body liquid. I was given water at this stop but it went right through me. My throat was raw from the vomiting. I was helped up and lowered to the ground from the train. I was on my feet but did not know if I could make the march to the compound, a distance of four kilometers. At this point I was carrying nothing, only the rags on my back.

After detraining, the column started to march to Marlag und Milag Nord, prisoner of war camps for the Royal Navy and merchant seamen. The Red Cross had already condemned Marlag Nord as unfit and unsanitary.

My comrades were helping me when a horse drawn wagon with a guard driver hauling German kits and supplies arrived. A member of our group approached the German driver and in German begged him to allow me to lie in the back of the wagon, like on a tail gate of a pickup. They gave him ten packs of cigarettes and he consented. Being on the wagon I moved up to the head of the column and reached the gate ahead of the main column. The driver told the guards at the gate that I was ill and should go to the infirmary. They told him no as they had orders to keep the prisoners at the gate until they received further orders.

I got off the wagon and sat on the ground, and in the rain waited for the main column that arrived shortly thereafter. I could not have weighed more than 130 pounds at this point.

According to my records, the head of the column reached the camp at about 1900 hours. It was then learned that a personal search of each prisoner was to be made before he entered the barrack area. This was to start at once and batches of twenty being searched at a time, and each search lasting twenty minutes. At this rate the search would take more than twenty hours for the column to enter the camp. The reply was that they had their orders and though eventually the time of search was reduced to a point where it became perfunctory, it was continued. Not until 0130 hours on the 5th of February that the last of the prisoners reached the barracks.

Meanwhile I was waiting for our group outside. It was raining hard and I and others were all standing in mud tracks covered with pools of water. It was impossible to keep anything dry. Several collapsed and were taken to the hospital. I was admitted and also taken to the hospital. I did not want to go until I had met up with our group, but I had no choice. Almost all of the prisoners were sick, most from exhaustion after the march and train journey. Many were suffering from frostbite, dysentery, and vomiting. Indeed for the majority, this wait after eight days of movement under conditions described proved the breaking point. More than seventy percent of the camp suffered from gastritis, dysentery, colds, influenza, and other illnesses during the first week. The strength of the column on arrival was 1,916 officers and other ranks. We lost along the way about eighty or eighty-five, not necessarily dead, but no longer with us. I am sure a large percent of those did indeed die.

The camp hospital was a shambles. There was no medical equipment, no sheets, nothing, only concrete floors and filthy bathrooms, no hot water for two or three days. I do not remember ever seeing a doctor. I was now going to the bathroom more than ever, and I had the chills so bad that I could not stop shaking. I would get in the cot and wrap myself in the blanket trying to get control of my body. I was so thin that I did not recognize myself in a reflection in a window. I thought it was someone on the outside.

My clothes were disgusting and when I saw a German orderly, I asked him if I could get my clothes washed. He said no, so I offered him ten packages of cigarettes, which I did not have. He took all my clothes, even my underwear. I was naked with only a double blanket hoping that my clothes would indeed come back. Al from our group visited me and I told him I needed ten packs of cigarettes. He said, "No problem. But what I am here for is to tell you we've saved your spot with us in the barracks." I felt better hearing that and thanked him and he left. The orderlies were giving us some kind of liquid for the dysentery and the vomiting had stopped.

My clothes came back the next day. I was very thankful for that; they had shrunk a little, but so had I. So they fit fine. They were feeding us hot soup in the so-called hospital and that gave me a little strength. After about a week, I requested to be released and they were happy to get rid of me. I told the orderly I would return with his cigarettes. He got alarmed and asked my barracks and room number and said he would be by, as he would be in trouble if the officer in charge found out.

The accommodations available consisted of twelve wooden living huts, two kitchens, two washhouses, and two latrines. The latrines were the same as Sagan, a shed, a wooden floor, and in the center were a rectangular pit about five feet deep and four feet by ten feet in size. Around the rectangle was a rail off the floor about 18" high. You sat on the backs of your thighs so that your bottom was clear and did you business, praying that you did not fall in.

The previous tenants had been the Royal Navy and Gurkas from India. The huts had been gutted. There was neither light nor stoves in many rooms and no movable equipment in the kitchens. There were only beds for 460 people and no straw mattresses. There was an assortment of small benches and small tables. Wood straw was provided for sleeping purposes but it was damp. Our group must have moved fast as we did have bunks. I think they commandeered them from other barracks as they were in the first group to be entered into the camp.

The camp was unfit for occupation; the German authority was trying, I believe, to supply what was necessary. It never came to pass before we were on the road again. The most important item (after food) was fuel. So prisoners were still trying to dry clothes weeks after occupation.

We had an added strain on endurance caused by the German Security who kept the whole camp in rain and cold for prolonged and unnecessary periods in order to establish numbers. This could have been done in half the time inside the barrack blocks.

We set up housekeeping once more and scrounging

again became necessary using cigarettes as barter. We were able to have one German get us a table and a few chairs. The place was alive with lice and for some reason I was not bothered. Doug Wraith, who slept in the bunk below me, was a mess with lice bites. Red Cross parcels started coming in again and I was starting to build up my strength. There was a high bar located close to our block. Every day I would go out and try to chin myself. I never had the strength. In fact, I never was able to do it again in captivity, because of the complete deterioration of my body from the effects of the forced march and dysentery. My body was going to take a long time to regain its strength.

As things settled down, we again were on monthly delousing. It was on one of these trips that I noticed farmers or perhaps laborers digging up beets. So on our way back I stopped just inside the gate and the guard did not seem to mind. I beckoned to one of the workers and made gestures to make a trade for some beets for cigarettes. We made the trade and I was feeling good as I brought them back to the room. So we cooked them and ate. The results were terrible; they were sugar beets for cattle and our stomachs were not able to assimilate these. I went into cramps and dysentery again. I was miserable for about a week. Even today I have to be very careful as the virus is still there.

It was late February before I was able to gain some strength, not much though. The weather was terrible, cold and snowy and very little sun. The Allies were now breaking out and there was word that the British Second Army was heading our way. Surely they would not move us again. We got a report that the Russians were now forty miles from Berlin and the Americans had passed the Siegfried line.

There was but one shower in the camp, located in the

ablution shed, which was largely open to the weather. It consisted of one wall and a tin roof. It had a shower of sorts. The water was ice cold and the concrete floor made for frigid conditions. After the initial shock of freezing water had subsided, then you did the usual in and out dashing that I mentioned earlier.

By the 6th of February officialdom had raised its precise head once more. A veneer of organization had permeated the camp. The Germans now reverted to strict discipline and we were again subject to many appell calls for numbers count.

I want to mention that there were over a hundred men on sick call the second day we entered this camp. The sick bay was full to the four walls, a few patients lying on cots—I was fortunate to be one. The rest were on the floor covered with greatcoats and blankets. The haggard appearance of all was apparent in the abnormal preponderance of unshaven beards. We had all lost so much weight and that brings on the sunken eye sockets and bony faces.

In addition to the torrential rain that we had on the night of our arrival, the deluge continued for the next two or more weeks. The rain penetrated broken windows and roofs leaked like a sieve. Firewood was non-existent. So a log ration was issued of one wet stump per block. It broke up into barely enough chips for each room to cook one hot meal.

Our camp was called Marlag M. There was no main gate as it opened onto the German Vorlager. This separated us from the naval compounds; naval prisoners had been the previous tenants and were moved to accommodate us. There was a barbed wire fence that separated us from the Vorlager. The camp had the usual double barbed wire with coils of the same in between.

We had finished our supply of food from Sagan. A

shipment of Red Cross parcels arrived from Lubeck about 130 kilometers distant and half parcels were to begin again. The weather turned cold and I stayed in bed the rest of that day.

About February 11th the goons were frustrated. The total prisoner count was apparently four men less than the Luftwaffe claimed to have handed over upon their departure, so the huts had to be searched and identity cards checked. We stood in the saturated sand of the parade ground in the pouring rain. The following day was a repeat standing three or four hours in the cold rain. The smell of wet clothing, damp socks, and squelching boots was inescapable. It had rained but for a few breaks each day and night for two weeks since our arrival.

I started getting nauseated again and remained in bed after the appell; I was still so miserably weak. I decided to join the sick parade. A small chubby German naval officer, who may have been a doctor, asked me to strip and did a lot of thumping on my chest and back. He commented on my loss of weight. Sighing, he needled my arm and withdrew blood. He lit a cigarette and I got dressed. And he casually mentioned that although he hoped it was merely bronchitis, he could hear something that might prove more serious. He wrote my name down, poured me a spoonful of cough syrup and told me to go to bed. No return trip was required, he said.

You know, it reminded me of the toothache I had in Sagan. When I went to the so-called dentist they pulled it out without Novocain. It was a molar, and I still have the space in my mouth where it was pulled. All they did was deaden the gum on the outside of the tooth.

The morning following the sick call I thought I would walk the circuit of the camp. While attempting this my legs began to fail me and I tottered back to bed. Weakness was commonplace throughout the camp. The rigors of the march and no food had sapped our strength. I can recall that just slicing bread caught me panting and needing to rest.

We got a few books from the Navy camp next door. I got one, title "Devil's Creek". I think I went to "bed" to read and stay warm. Our clothes would not dry in this weather and when we saw the sun for brief moments it appeared weak.

It started to snow again in February, a wet snow. So the days passed and I moved very slowly and would stay under covers as much as possible. My arms and neck were now strikingly thin, my ribs very evident and the hollow between neck and collarbone cup size. I did finally shave, although I have a light beard it was quite long and straggly. I felt better.

We had a bad incident happen. One of our guys was trading with a guard for some food. He stepped over the warning wire and the tower guard shot him. Black market trading still went on however.

The first part of March 50,000 American food parcels were reported to have arrived from Lubeck, and full parcel issue was to begin the following week. American food parcels contained cigarettes (unlike the Canadian and British). This was good news not only for the food, but we needed the cigarettes for bartering.

The rain and snow continued and ended in a deep freeze. While lying in our bunks, we used to torture ourselves with conversation centered on favorite meals. Then as compensation for the cold, we voted for another raid on the dwindling rations for a slice of bread and goon jam.

We were now without lights every other night, due to the local power plant being bombed. We used margarine lamps, which created foul smoke that offset the value of their feeble flicker of light.

In the second week or so, after five weeks of rain and snow, the sun appeared. I remember our group behind the block, out of the wind, sitting in the sun, grabbing the sun's rays and absorbing them into our bodies like water into a sponge. The full parcel issue of the past week was a blessing, renewing our strength while replenishing our cigarette supply.

During the second or third week we were witnesses to a large-scale air raid on Hamburg. It was a night raid. It was later reported that 1,250 aircraft participated, only losing thirteen. It began about 10:30 p.m., ringing the camp from east to west through north and continuing past midnight. We only counted nine planes being shot down during the raid. It was freezing cold but we stayed out and watched it. Then a few days later in daylight, about 850 Flying Fortresses and Liberators flew directly over the camp at about 12,000 feet in perfect formation. No flak or fighter opposition was observed.

During this time we had news that the Allies had crossed the Rhine River and another invasion had landed on the Dutch coast. We immediately became concerned about another forced march.

Along about the third week of March, German rations (bread and potato) again were reduced. As long as the parcels continued to come, however, we could manage. To make it worse there was a decree from the kommandant that all Red Cross food in tin cans must be emptied into open receptacles before being issued. Such action prevented planned rationing because of the need for quick consumption to prevent spoilage. The reason given was that the Third Reich needed the tin. Our senior British officer refused to accept these conditions and the camp agreed to support his position with a forty-eight hour hunger strike. In my condition, this was all I needed, but naturally I agreed to go along—as if I had a choice. In addition we needed all the cans to make utensils.

A second meeting with the kommandant resulted in a refusal. Two days later the hunger strike was over, and we lost the basic point, for all tinned food was being emptied. But obtaining food in any condition whatsoever was a victory at that moment. We needed food desperately; I had blacked out while standing and smashed the small table in the room. We needed the firewood anyhow. As I regained consciousness, I heard the familiar engine sounds of aircraft approaching. I got up and went outside to see about 120 Lancasters approaching the camp. They turned into their bombing run directly overhead and disappeared to the southwest on a course for Bremen, leaving a profound silence.

The sun was showing itself more and we started having full days of sunshine. The days and nights were starting to play more on our psyches; the enervating atmosphere of prison camp was all pervading. It penetrated your thoughts, into the spoken word, and into visions. All you saw was run down decaying old wood, faded blue clothing, damp images, and mist at dusk and cold gray. The bunks were filled with quiet figures, the flicker of a margarine lamp, the flare of a cigarette, and creaks of the bunk as a body turned seeking comfort. March turned to April.

April 5th, 1945, my twenty-second birthday, was celebrated by the sight of a V-2 rocket fired from a point northeast of the camp. There was a prolonged roar and a flash of white flame. Later the camp was surrounded by flares dropped by aircraft, over a circumference of several miles that lasted for about hour and a half. We thought that it was paratroops dropping in the vicinity. Then, close to midnight, we saw flares over Hamburg. For over forty-five minutes we watched the most spectacular raid of our imprisonment, huge sheet-like explosions of flame illuminating towering columns of smoke, which rose from beyond the brilliantly lit horizon. We did not hear any sound probably due to the wind direction. It was as though we were the audience to a film without soundtrack.

There was a lot of tension in the camp, as the sounds of bombs and artillery became closer and more frequent in the vicinity. Field Marshall Montgomery had been advancing very fast and we felt he could reach us by the next day. He was less than fifty miles from Bremen and pressing on rapidly. I noticed a guard had a suitcase in the ditch alongside him. It was the first inkling on my part that the Germans might be ready to take off because of the proximity of the allied forces.

One of my group received a letter on that day. This was the first mail since our arrival two months prior. I was feeling stronger, but was still unable to chin myself.

We witnessed numerous V-2 rockets being fired almost daily. Fighter aircraft strafing was also heard daily.

On April 8th or thereabouts all appells had been cancelled. There had been no light in camp for forty-eight hours and water was available one hour a day in three twenty-minute periods. We were advised to fill every available container, as there would likely be no further supply after 6 p.m.

There was a large amount of movement on the road, tanks pulling cannons as well as ambulances and staff cars, all liberally camouflaged with leaf-covered branches. Montgomery's Desert Rats had advanced to twenty-two miles southwest of Bremen. If they made a drive to Bremen, they would cut off our sole line of retreat in event of another march—but no such luck.

On April 9th at 7:30 p.m. we prepared to leave camp. During an appell at 2:30, we were ordered to prepare for departure at 6:30 p.m. "Failure to comply would result in the use of force," we were told.

Following the issue of two complete food parcels per man, we ate as we packed. My pack was overflowing and the thought of carrying it haunted me. I knew I would have to jettison much of what I carried. I was still too weak to carry any more than twenty or thirty pounds for a prolonged distance and time.

We understood that the British were now only twelve miles from Bremen. A group of prisoners broke into the kitchen in order to obtain white flour, soap, and dried soup. They then spread these supplies over the sand of the parade ground, forming POW and RAF in huge letters and indicating our likely route with a large arrow.

On the 10th we departed in dense fog, only to be stopped a hundred yards beyond the gate. The Kommandant was nervous due to an air raid going on and the fog so he returned us to the camp. Our rooms were in shambles but we made the best of it. Then we repacked and left the Marlag M and Tarmstedt at nine o'clock in the morning. Some had made carts that broke down after the first few miles; the problem was with the hubs and wheels.

The column took to ditches two or three times during the day because of air alerts. We were privy to watching two British Tempest fighters shooting up unknown targets a few fields away.

We were ordered into a field the first night out. This must have been the 11th of April. The group ahead of us noticed haystacks and ran to retrieve some hay for sleeping purposes. A guard screamed at them, leveled his rifle, and shot in the middle of them. One of the prisoners was shot through the inside of his left thigh about two inches from the groin and grazing his right knee, and the bullet lodged in the ankle of another

136

prisoner.

Our commanding officer protested, and an ambulance was summoned and the lads were taken to the hospital. They seemed in good spirits; the Germans were very trigger happy and extremely nervous. That night the noise of heavy transports on the road made for a restless sleep. I awoke to a heavy fog. An appell was attempted on the road and we moved off.

The fog dispersed by noon, and we continued on, with frequent breaks. Later that day we pitched camp across from a boiler works where hot water was available. Having traded for some eggs with the locals, we had a warm snack. I used a blanket for a tent and slept until morning

On April the 12th, the sun-brilliant morning was dulled by the news that two men were killed and seven wounded yesterday by Allied aircraft strafing the column to the rear of our position. The Allies were further south and therefore we were not to be rescued soon. The day was nice, however, and we only marched until 2:30, which helped our spirits. Then later a pair of British Tempest fighters shot up our field as we all jumped into ditches that surrounded us; there were no casualties. We stayed an extra day at this location. The Germans did provide us with an issue of canned meat and we decided to make a stew of sorts. We went to collect firewood, but were shot at by a guard, so we ate it cold.

We left at approximately 9:30 on the 14th of April, the route taking us through rolling hills and lush farming area. The guards seemed relaxed, so we took advantage of trading with the locals. I was communicating with a lady and her young daughter. The young girl spoke good English and said that they would give me a can of food if I wrote them a letter saying that we had helped them. I was puzzled; I really did not get the drift. Then I realized that they were afraid that when the Americans came they would all be killed; the German newspapers had used this propaganda on the public. They handed me a paper pad and I wrote, "These are kind people. They helped us and gave us food; treat them well." I signed it Flying Officer Stuart G. Hunt. I often wonder if that note is still in existence. I am sure that I would not be able to recognize the farm. They then gave me a number ten can with no label on it, and I thanked them.

The German guard who was watching the transaction then came up to me and demanded the can. I pulled away from his outstretched hand and began walking in the column. The woman and the girl started to scream at him with threatening fingers. I took advantage of this to get lost in the column, and caught up with my group. I kept the can to myself, however. I shook the can but it did not feel like loose soup or canned tomatoes, so with the little can openers that are part of the contents in our Red Cross parcels I opened the can about quarter turn and sucked not knowing what I was about to taste.

Can you imagine my surprise? It was a can of sweetened condensed milk, and I never tasted anything so delicious. I finished the can right then and there *myself*. I vowed that when I got out of this mess I would always have "condagers" as I called it, and to this day I love it. (Great on graham crackers; keep the can in the freezer and it spreads nice and thick.) Later I was able to make a trade ten cigarettes for eight eggs. I was feeling better and actually putting on a pound or so of muscle weight due to the walking and the weight I was carrying.

The news of Roosevelt's death came as a shock and created unanimous expressions of sorrow. The Allies were reported to be seventy-six miles southwest of Hamburg. Our guards had already surrendered, in spirit, if not in fact. I believe the last town was called Horneburg.

Another Camp and March

The Elbe River was ahead of us about sixteen kilometers and the weather had turned cold again. The thought of being ferried across the river caused me concern as the Allied aircraft were shooting everything that moved. Being out in the middle of a river a mile wide was not my idea of a good day. We reached the Elbe and the ferry carried about seventy prisoners per trip and the crossing took about twenty minutes. We made the crossing and walked through flat marshy terrain and arrived in a town called Jork, I think. We were to wait until the column reformed after the river crossing.

It was here in the town that this incident happened. We were sitting on the paved road and on one side there was a beer garden and on the other side a bakery. Other businesses lined each side of this small village. I said to Dave, a member of our group, "I am going to try and trade for some bread in the bakery. Do you have anything besides cigarettes?" He answered, "I have a little coffee."

The guards were relaxed, so I took the coffee and went into the bakery. The man looked at me. I showed him the coffee, and then pointing at the bread, I said in my best German, "Bread for coffee." He replied, "Ja," and handed me a loaf. I gave him the coffee and left with a loaf of bread about fifteen inches long. I returned to Dave and we broke the bread in half. The guards still did not appear to notice or didn't care to notice.

I asked Dave, "How about a beer?" "Fine," was the reply, so we walked into the beer garden and the waiter or proprietor approached the table. We were not in the main barroom; we were sitting outside on the terrace. I said to him in German, "Ten cigarettes for two beers." He replied, "Ja," and went off to get the beer. There were two German panzer soldiers inside the beer hall who saw us. They waved in a friendly manner and must have told the barkeep to give us the beer on them, because when the beer was brought they raised their glass with salutations, and we replied. We had about four swallows of beer and a few bites of the fresh warm bread when who should walk by but the major kommandant. He was in shock to see us sitting there, drew his revolver, and in a loud voice routed us out of there. I did manage another gulp of beer, however.

Well, the guards caught hell and for the balance of the day were more alert. As the column had now completed the river crossing and regrouped, we were on the move again. As the order to march was given, the proprietor of the beer hall ran out and handed me two bottles of beer and requested the ten cigarettes, which I gave him. So we rejoiced, but apparently I paid too much as others told me they bartered one beer for one cigarette.

The sweetened condensed milk played hell with my tender stomach and the beer did not help matters, but it seemed like everything I ate was a problem. We got a hold of some rhubarb and that was tough. I had stomach cramps so severe that I would double up in pain.

The next week we made many stops, camping and trying to stay dry at night. One night we slept in a pigsty; it was the only place that was out of the rain. We got no sleep, of course, as the pigs grunted and snorted all night, but we were dry.

Around the 20th of April, we reached a town named Elhemhorst in deteriorating weather conditions, heavy winds and downpour. We had only been on the march ten days, but our bodies were telling us it was months. We understood that the Allies were only twenty miles away, but we had been anticipating liberation for so long that by now we were very skeptical of any news. Our group was trying to stay ahead of the main column, because the opportunity was better for bartering. There was always a race from others to pass us. The problem was the SS troops who were scouring the neighborhood to round up prisoners ahead of the main party. We were warned and decided to wait for the main body.

On or about April 22nd we were told that we were to make camp in a field adjacent to a farmhouse until further notice. There was a small pond on the property that gave us an opportunity to wash some clothes and ourselves. We were on the outskirts of Lubeck and it did not appear that there was any direction that we could be moved at the moment. There were no facilities to accommodate over 1,900 prisoners. Our group located next to the pond and made makeshift shelters. We started up housekeeping again. The area was quite pretty before the horrible mess the prisoners were making. The farmer complained bitterly about all the destruction we were doing, and rightfully so. Our group captain tried to placate him, but the fact that his chickens and other live stock were disappearing hardly sufficed. The area was rolling hills and the guards were very nervous. We noticed that many suitcases were in storage on the wagon with their supplies.

The major was able to commandeer 4,000 Red Cross food parcels from the Red Cross headquarters in Lubeck. So we had food for a couple of weeks. The number of guards seemed to be dwindling. Dave and I climbed up a knoll and we could see the Hamburg-Lubeck autobahn. Each day we would go up and look. Weather was good and late spring was kind to us.

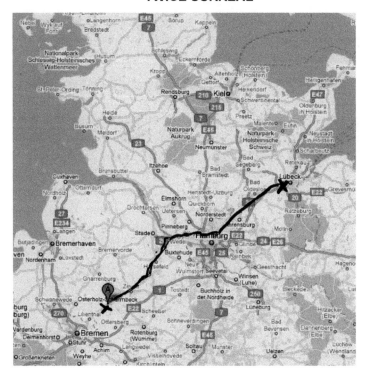

Tarmstedt to Lubeck, 90 miles: On the 14th of April we were order to march again. We had no idea where we were headed, but not west toward the Allies. Our heading was north-east. As we all speculated, we finally ended up just a few miles south of Lubeck.

We were very fortunate as the weather turned milder, not like the first march, where the weather was mostly below zero and blizzard conditions.

The route took us north of Hamburg. We had to cross the Elbe River. On our arrival near Lubeck, we bivouacked in a farmer's field until the British Second Army liberated us.

Forced March

R.A.F. Pilot Took Secret Pictures
of Canadian POW's in Germany.

Forced March (Concluded)

WARNING SIGN to prevent the British shelling the ... was put up by prisoners near Lubeck. In back- ...nd are seen the barns of the Trenth...

These newspaper accounts speak for themselves. Due to the strafing by our own planes and ground shelling, we put up signs hoping they would be noticed.

AW SIGNALS spelling out R.A.F. were spread on surrounding fields for Allied
ter recognition. Prisoners had experienced bombing and strafing from our planes,
e anxious to avoid repetition.

Above is a newspaper photo of our last camp. There was a small pond that had some fish. The farmer who owned the farm was not happy that we were camped there. We did make a mess. What can you expect with 2000 prisoners with no facilities?

Another Camp and March

This is another photo of our last confinement before we were liberated by the British 2nd army.

LIBERATION

On May 3 1945, Dave and I took our usual walk up the knoll. We noticed that there were no guards, maybe one who we shook off, and continued up the knoll. Upon reaching the top for the view of the autobahn, lo and behold, what a sight! Every lane on both sides, approaching, was filled with British armored vehicles of all descriptions moving at a rapid pace. We jumped like children and shouted to the prisoners below. "They're here! They're here! The British are here!" Hundreds of prisoners rushed up the hill and rejoiced, tears flowing freely with hugging and shouting. It was the most magnificent sight. Men cried like babies; some had been incarcerated many years. In our group, two had been prisoners for over five years, two for over three, two for more than two, and two others for more than a year.

I made my way down to the camp and over to where the German guards had a billet. There inside the barn were uniforms and weapons; they had indeed changed into civilian clothes during the night and left. I took two Lugers, a German submachine gun, two helmets, and some other souvenirs. I put them in one of the backpacks left there, hid them, and came back for the items later.

After I hid my cache, a British command car drove into the camp, occupied by two British Tommies. A roar went up as we all gathered around the car.

"Where are you going?" I asked one.

"To Lubeck," was the reply.

"Good! Then can I come?" I asked.

"Sure," they answered.

Four of us hopped into the command car. The Tommie gave assurance to the rest of the prisoners that the main body would be along shortly and with that we drove off, heading north to Lubeck, a few miles away.

When we entered Lubeck the streets were deserted. Seeing a beer garden, the driver asked us if with would care for a beer. We replied in the affirmative and with that we entered the beer garden. The proprietor saw the uniforms of the Brits, ran out of the room, and disappeared. So the Tommie hopped over the bar and, playing bartender, supplied us with bottles of beer. We sat and drank and talked about the war for about thirty minutes. It was then time for them to leave and they informed us that they would not be able to furnish transportation back to camp.

With that one of the soldiers left the room and returned in a few minutes saying that there was a German Opel in the garage and that we should use it for our return trip. If it needed gas, the Tommies said they would be able to spare a few gallons from the extra gas they were carrying. Then they discovered the wine cellar and told us to load up and take it back to camp. We loaded the wine into the car and headed back to camp. They had to give us a push, because the battery was dead in the Opel.

Off we went. The driver was obviously drunk on a couple of beers and had also been drinking some wine. We told him to slow down. As we neared the camp we had to leave the paved road; the ruts were deep. The driver lost control and rolled the car, smashing all the wine bottles. It was a mess and we all stunk of booze. Fortunately and remarkably, no one was seriously hurt. We left the car wheels up and walked to the camp dejected that we were unable to complete the mission.

I returned to the group and they informed me that we had been ordered to stay in this camp, and that we were not allowed to wander. I thought to myself we are free but we are now prisoners of our own troops. Of course, it was for our own safety, and consolidation was important for logistic purposes. We were informed that they hoped to be able to start our return to the UK in three days.

It was the 6th of May 1945, I think. I kept thinking about the Opel down the road and getting back to Lubeck for another try at the wine cellar. We now had British troops in the camp as it was imperative that we did not wander all over the countryside. It was their job to keep the prisoners in a group as there was no specified time for the trucks to arrive to repatriate us. I rounded up five others and assured them that this would be a fast trip. There being no wire around the camp, it was easy to leave. We located the car, righted it, and exhausted ourselves pushing it to start it. Finally, it started; I drove and headed to Lubeck.

There was a lot of activity on the road, tanks and troops. We worked our way up to the front and located the beer garden, went inside, and the place was cleaned out. We tried the draft barrels and got about half glass of beer. Apparently, the Brits had quenched their thirst.

The Opel was still running, but was banged up, so we pushed it back in the garage and went out on the street to see if there was anything of interest. There was some gunfire up the road and a tank pulled the lid down and moved in the direction of the small arms fire, and "WHAM" his cannon belched and a house became history. No more gunfire.

Military police in a Jeep stopped us. They wanted to know if we were from the camp up north or south. We told them south. They told us to climb aboard, that their orders were to take us back. They said, "Sorry, lads, trucks are on the way to take you to an airport for your return to the UK." So back we went, all six in a jeep, eight including the two Military Police.

Back at the camp it was another two days before the trucks arrived. There were open stake trucks and we were crowded but we did not care. We waved to everyone and shouted back and forth to the passing traffic. This time we crossed the Elbe River on a pontoon bridge and that was an experience as the floating bridge swayed back and forth. Our arrival at the airport was greeted with another delousing and then food. We were cautioned not to overeat. Actually, I don't think we were able to, as our stomachs had shrunk. We had a hot shower and clean clothes were issued. We each had a clean bunk and then went to sleep.

The next day paperwork was filled out, and aircraft assignment by number for the trip back to Britain. I was to leave the next day, aboard a Lancaster aircraft converted for troop and cargo. We landed at a Typhoon fighter station in Lincolnshire. The aircraft taxied to a prescribed stop alongside several large tents, the engines stopped, and the door was opened. We were confronted with a white rope corridor leading across the grass.

Liberation

Following it, I walked into the shaded interior of a tent, where I was immediately seized and firmly placed prone on a bench. Efficient hands sprayed white power up my pant legs, down my waist, up my sleeves and down my neck. Equally efficiently, I was placed on my feet and guided into an adjoining tent, where a doughnut was placed in one hand, and a cup of tea in the other. A motherly woman appeared before me. "How are you, lad?" she asked. I stared at her mutely, but I was smiling.

I remained at this RAF station a very short time, a couple of hours perhaps. Three buses pulled up in front of the building where we were completing additional paperwork. We were given a shot in the arm, and I don't remember what it was for. I was assigned billet in the Royal Bath Hotel in Bournemouth and instructed to board the bus.

The trip down was very raucous and joyful. The impact of freedom was starting to penetrate. You could feel the mood on the bus. Most of the prisoners were talking about food, pubs, and girls. We made a lot of stops for obvious reasons; buses then did not have toilet facilities. It also gave us time for a Bitters beer, carried back on the bus. It was remarkable how fast you can forget the devastating conditions you were part of. One could not conceive that these busloads of airmen were prisoners of war a few days ago. Youth, I wonder? All I could think of was getting out and walking freely through the streets of Bournemouth.

The bus pulled up in front of the hotel and as I stepped down, sitting there on the steps of the hotel was Jim Horwood. I was taken aback. I said, "Jim, Jim! What are you doing here?"

"Waiting for you! I've been here for a week waiting for your return. What the hell took you so long?"

TWICE SURREAL

I had no idea that Jim had also been shot down. I learned that their plane had ditched. Jim and his crew made it to shore and were helped by a Dutch family, remaining in the house for about four or five months. The British liberated them.

I was delighted of course to be reunited with my old buddy. He looked very good; I was as skinny as a rake. We were billeted in the same hotel, the Royal Bath. Jim would be returning home before me, due to the fact that he had been liberated about three or four weeks prior. Well, we would worry about that when the time came. Today was all that counted. After checking in with the sergeant, I was informed that I was to report to the infirmary for possible hospitalization due to my undernourished condition. I was mad as hell. I thought, I am going to be a prisoner again. I told Jim, "I will be right back." I left the building, and with directions from the sergeant located the infirmary.

There were about four or five others in a waiting room. I walked up to the nurse and asked her if I could see the doctor. She told me I would have to wait my turn. I showed her the slip that was handed to me by the sergeant. She noticed that I was a returning prisoner, and told me to wait. She returned almost immediately and told me the doctor would see me. The others in the room gave me a dirty look. I can only guess that they were not POWs.

The doctor took one look at me and said, "You need to be hospitalized so that we can fatten you up. You are meatless." We went back and forth and I told him that I could get just as fat on the outside as in. I said that I had been incarcerated for so long that it would break my spirit if I could not be with my friends. He finally relented and made me promise to return every day, without exception, for vitamin shots and boosters or something. I said, "Yes, anything." Well, I never saw him again and I am sure that with all the prisoners he had to contend with I was not missed.

I was back and Jim could not believe that I was free. I was issued a new battle dress uniform. They even had volunteers to sew on the necessary insignias. So by 8 p.m. Jim and I were ready to hit the town. With an issue of advance pay we headed for the pubs. Oh, yes—prior to leaving the hotel, I was able to send a telegram to my parents that I was safe, back in England.

The city was filled with returning POWs and all the pubs were overflowing with the freedom and the end of the war. We did our share and got so rowdy that the proprietor called the Bobbies and we were escorted to the paddy wagon. The police were good and knew that we had just been reborn. They drove us back to the hotel and told us to sober up. I recalled waking up in the morning feeling ill from booze, but the shocking discovery was that my souvenir bag of German trophies had been stolen. There was no finding the culprits and all the investigation proved fruitless. Needless to say I was very disappointed, but life moved on.

All my personal clothing had been sent to the Jenkins family in Welling, Kent. I made arrangements with Jim for a trip to retrieve my belongings. I had never met these people. I was unaware that my folks had been in touch with them and had been sending food parcels to them for over a year. We, Jim and I, managed to get a few oranges, some sugar, and a few other staples. I needed to take something to them as food was rationed.

By train we journeyed to London, then switched to a train to Welling. We had never visited this town before. It was very typically British, with row after row of narrow granite units with common walls. I noticed a flower shop where we bought some flowers and got directions to the street where the Jenkinses lived.

TWICE SURREAL

As we entered the street, about halfway down there was a banner stretched across the street. As we walked down, looking for the correct house address, we were able to read the printing on the banner, it said, "Welcome home, Canadians, to Aunt Ole's." I was really taken aback and confess that my eyes were wet. I was so moved that people I had never met could be so caring and generous, and take the trouble to show their appreciation by stringing a banner. I was very touched.

We found the address and went up a few stairs; I knocked on the door. A woman appeared and, throwing her arms around me, said, "You must be Stuart!" Her voice was so loving and tears were flowing down her cheeks.

"Oh come in, come in," she said, at the same time shouting to the rest of the family, "Stuart's here! Come on down and greet him!"

The whole Jenkins family—her husband, her sister (who worked as a mail carrier), and her son and daughter—gathered and after the initial introductions of Jim and me, we settled in with tea and sandwiches. Mrs. Jenkins told me that I was to call her "Auntie" and that we were not to have any notion about leaving that day or night. Her husband hauled out the beer that they have been saving, the sister started playing the piano, and we all started singing. Auntie had told me that she had informed my parents about hoping to have me stay with them at least a night. I was very pleased that my parents had been sending food. Frankly, the Jenkins family had very little—they lived in a small two story flat, but they had hearts as big as a mansion.

About six or seven in the evening Auntie mentioned to Jim and me that we should go outside for some reason I can't recall. So we did and as we stepped out the door a roar and clapping resounded. There were lights strung across the street and tables set out, a piano, and all the neighbors on the street. We danced and sang until the wee hours. It was the most memorable experience and has remained with me to this day.

When I returned to the United States, my wife and I continued to send parcels to the Jenkinses. Then the sad news reached us, in about 1948, the whole family over a period of a year had died of tuberculosis. I remain very grateful. God has them now.

Another extraordinary experience was that I and others had an invitation to Buckingham Palace for tea, to meet with the King George VI, the queen, and the two princesses, Elizabeth and Margaret. We made the journey to London and in the courtyard chatted with the Royals. The event was for Prisoners of War of the British Allied Services, to show appreciation for the sacrifices made.

It was shortly after the Buckingham Palace visit Jim shipped home and I was waiting for a ship assignment. The wounded had priority and then us. There were many wounded, so I did not get a ship until the end of June. The ship was the Louis Pasteur, a French liner. It was very crowded with wounded. Our accommodations were poor and the crossing seemed long, five days. We docked in Halifax, Nova Scotia, in early July 1945.

From Halifax we traveled by train to Montreal. On arrival, I was given forty-five days leave and the option for discharge or service in the Pacific. I opted for continued service and was to report back to Toronto for assignment to the Pacific Theatre, as the war was still raging with the Japanese.

As I was about to leave the train station, after buying a ticket to Detroit to see my parents, standing at the exit was my aunt, Gertie Stuart. She was such a kind and loving person and here she was alone to greet me. She insisted that I accompany her home overnight, before my trip to Detroit. She assured me that my parents knew that she was going to meet me, and I was to telephone them from the house. We hopped a cab and drove to her home. On arrival at my aunt's, Uncle Leslie was asleep as usual, and I did not awaken him. Young Leslie, my cousin, who was then about fourteen or fifteen, was there. So after a much-appreciated dinner, I needed to get to bed. She wanted me to take hers; I refused and slept on the couch while she stayed up doing my wash. She was a sweet lady and I loved her. I left in the morning for the train station and on to Detroit.

On arriving in Detroit, having called my parents previously with the time of arrival, my mother, dad, and brother Tom were all there to welcome me home. After all the tears and hugs, we drove to our home in Dearborn. I was informed that we would be leaving in the morning as my grandfather Hunt was critically ill and wanted to see me. I was very attached to my grandparents. Grandpa Hunt was always kind to me and I was told he wanted to see me before he died.

We drove back to Verdun, Quebec. I saw my grandfather and he wanted to hug me but was too weak. He spoke my name and I felt the love he had for me, and the concern that he must have felt in my absence. He died four hours later. I cried openly. He was the best grandpa a child could ever hope for.

We only had a week as my dad was still in the Army Air Corps and had to report back to his station in Willow Run. On the return trip to Detroit, we did manage to stop in Kingston to see Pat Draper, the mid-upper gunner of my bomber crew, and his family. We stayed the night in their home.

Back in Detroit, Jim was also on leave. We got together every day and some of the escapades I will not go into but we were wild, trying to make up for our lost time. We were in a bar on Michigan Avenue when we heard the war was over in the Pacific, August 8th, 1945. The city went wild, the streets were full of people celebrating. If you had a uniform on you were hugged and kissed by strangers. It was an amazing moment in history that crosses my mind at the oddest times.

My leave up, I reported to RCAF headquarters in Toronto and was told that I could not be processed due to the influx of service men being discharged and was given another two or three weeks leave. With the added time, I decided with another former prisoner, who I knew in the Stalag, to go to the recreation area of Lake Muskogee in northern Ontario. We did and had a great time. On return to Toronto, I was discharged late September 1945 and headed home to Detroit.

A few weeks after my return to Detroit, my father resigned from the Army Air Corps and we headed west to San Diego. When we arrived, we stayed a few days with the Baxters, our previous neighbors, where we had lived in 1941-42. My parents found an apartment on Fourth Avenue a few days later.

I called Bridget the day we got back and that evening drove to her apartment on Voltaire Street. I was still in uniform and the dog Skippy greeted me at the bottom of the stairs, carrying on like he remembered me. Bridget, Madeline, and Mother Darsey greeted me. We had coffee and cinnamon toast and Madeline never stopped talking. Bridget walked me to the car and I gave her a big kiss and knew that this was the girl for me.

My father was working for the Veterans Administration. I applied and started working in the adjudication department. I wanted to go back to school, but I was still trying to get my feet on the ground. Bridget and I were dating on a regular basis, and dancing at the

Hotel Del Coronado to big bands, here and in Los Angeles. We were having fun. I was still quite wild and drinking more than I should. Still being rehabilitated, I guess, or so I told myself. I was also playing hockey. I took a commission in the National Guard.

My parents had set aside the money that I had sent home while in service, so when I got back I had a nice little nest egg, about five thousand dollars, which was quite a bit in those days. Bridget and I got engaged and were married May 4th, 1946.

I was still working for the VA, but I was transferred to Los Angeles, which I did not like and the commute was aggravating. There were no freeways then. I was thinking seriously about making a career with the government, and to advance I would need further education especially in law. So I enrolled in a graduate law school and attended for two years. On February 22, 1947, Patricia, our first child, was born when we still lived in the apartment next to my parents on Fourth Avenue, a one bedroom. We moved to a two-bedroom apartment on Voltaire Street, the same units where Bridget was living on my return to San Diego. On June 29, 1948, Susan joined the family.

Things were going along nicely. I was getting my teeth knocked out playing hockey with a few stitches occasionally being required on my head, so everything was normal in that arena. I was now working for Prudential Insurance Company. I was unable to get back to San Diego with the VA as they had reduced the office staff and the division where I was working was not included in San Diego.

Meanwhile I was in a National Guard unit. I was required to attend one two-week military exercise per year, plus once a month at Fort Rosecrans. This was "okay" as it gave us additional income.

I'm pictured here in front of the Royal Bath Hotel where we were billeted while awaiting return home in June 1945.

This picture was taken in Bournemouth, England after being liberated and returned to the U.K.

Left to right: me at age 22, my friend James Horwood, David Stubbs, and unknown F/L buddy.

Prior to our return home, some of the prisoners of war were invited to Buckingham Palace for a visit with King George VI and his family including his daughter Elizabeth.

I attended with my buddies Jim Horwood and David Stubbs.

ONCE MISSING, NOW SAFE.

F/O Stuart G. Hunt

g Officer Hunt, younger son of Capt. T. B. Hunt of
, and of Mrs. Hunt, of Dearborn, Michigan, and for
ity has arrived in England after release from a
er of war camp.

This short article appeared in the Dearborn, Michigan newspaper and announced my return to England.

Back home in Dearborn, Michigan, I am pictured here with my father, Capt. Thomas B. Hunt, U.S. Army Air Corps. It was taken in 1945.

Liberation

This is another photo at the same location in Dearborn, Michigan. It was July 1945 and I was on leave.

I had volunteered for duty in the Pacific, but the war ended in August 1945. I was therefore separated from the service in September 1945.

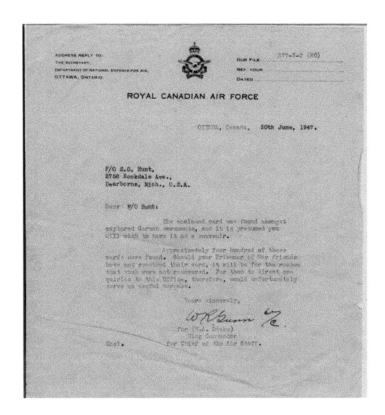

Sometime after having returned home, I received this letter forwarded to me by the RCAF.

Enclosed with it was my German POW registration card. It had been found with 400 of these cards (see registration card in next photo).

Liberation

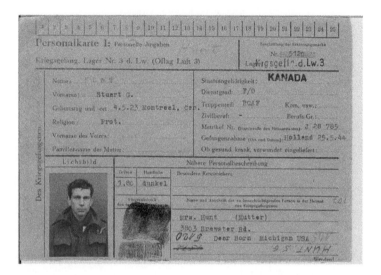

This was the registration card that the Germans apparently completed on prisoners of war.

After the war was over, 400 of these cards were found. This was forwarded to me by the RCAF (see letter in previous photo).

Congratulations . . .

It is indeed a pleasure to welcome you as a member of the Caterpillar Club.

As is customary, we have had the official insignia of the Club made for you. The insignia, together with the membership card which bears your name, is enclosed herewith.

These are presented to you with our compliments and best wishes, in recognition of the emergency parachute jump which you made.

IRVING AIR CHUTE CO., INC.

The requirements for membership are rigid – members *must* have saved their lives by jumping with a parachute. There are no annual fees or meetings. Members only get a pin and a membership card. The "golden caterpillar" award is a tiny gold lapel pin with amethyst eyes.

The club was founded by Irvin Airchute Company of Canada in 1922. The name "Caterpillar Club" makes reference to the silk threads that made the original parachutes thus recognizing the debt owed to the silk worm and the fact that the caterpillar lets itself down to earth by a silken thread.

Liberation

Thanks for the Memories, of flights to Germany
Across the Northern Sea, with blazing guns
We fought the Hun, for air supremacy.
How lucky we were!

Thanks for the memories, of Me-109's
And flak guns on the Rhine
They did their bit and we were hit
So ended our good times…we miss them so much!

We drifted far out of formation
We jumped – and what a sensation
And now we sweat out the duration
Our job is done, we had our fun.

So thanks for the memories
Of days we had to stay, at Stalag Luft 1A
The cabbage raw which had to do
Till Red Cross Parcels came
How thankful we were.

So thanks for the memories
When "D" Day came along
We changed our marching song
From "Forever and a Day" to "War ain't Here to Stay"
We thank God for that!

Sung to the tune of Bob Hope's theme song, "Thanks for the Memories". The author of this version is unknown. It is reported to have been written by a POW from Stalag Luft 1A.

Reported by the RAF Bomber Command website:

"From the 55 raids mounted by Bomber Command between the end of August 1943 and the end of March 1944 (roughly the period spanning the Battle of Britain), a staggering 1,578 aircraft failed to return. This represented an average rate of loss of 5% per raid, or twice the front line strength of the Command. This meant that only some 20 per cent of the bomber crews successfully managed to complete a tour of 30 operations in this period of the airwar."

KOREA

Did I say it was "okay"? Ever hear about the "little police action" in a country by the name of Korea? It started in 1950. Well, 58,000 individuals lost their lives in this "police action". Yes, you guessed it: our unit was one of the first units to be called up. Now I had a wife and two darling daughters who passed for twins and I get a return engagement. We had about a week before I was to report to Fort Lewis, Washington.

I remember well at the Santa Fe railroad station where the battalion boarded the train that would take us to Fort Lewis. A lot of friends showed up at the station, including some from Prudential, where I was now working, to wish me well. My wife and daughters were very sad, with tears welling in their eyes. I promised to have them with me as soon as possible. But I had no idea how I was going to do this.

After a week or so at Fort Lewis I was assigned as liaison to the Air National Guard. The firing center was in

Yakima, Washington. My job was to coordinate the Air Guard pulling windsocks for the anti-aircraft battalions to fire at and at times barely miss the plane. I was later informed that I had orders for Korea.

This meant that I would not be going overseas immediately, so I rented a small house near American Lake, south of Tacoma. (There was no vacant housing on the base at this time.) I then moved the family up from San Diego.

Actually, I reflect many times about our stay in Washington. I felt we had a happy time there. The children seem to fit right in with military life and we made close friends that remain with us today. We did move into "splinterville," housing on the base. We were all young families with lots of kids. We had time together except for when I was at the firing center in Yakima.

I received orders for duty in Korea. I was the first to receive orders; they needed forward observers—the reason obvious—cannon fodder. My MOS (military occupational specialty) filled the bill, I guess. One other fellow officer received orders on the same day. This was not good news for the family.

I had to move fast, as I wanted to get them settled in San Diego. The movers came and we took off for Southern California with very few stops as I had to find living quarters for the family before I left. I located a house on Poe Street in Point Loma. The place was filthy and the yard needed work. The ten days left was used to try and straighten the place out. The neighborhood was good, that is what I was concerned about. I was to report to Seattle for embarkation. First stop would be Japan, Camp Drake, and then Puson, Korea for assignment.

We were given numerous shots for God knows what, which continued on board the ship. We boarded the USS General M.C. Meigs. The crew were both civilian and

Korea

Navy. I crossed the 180th meridian at latitude 50° 01' and was duly initiated into the "Silent Mysteries of the Far East". Our quarters were excellent and so was the food we received in the officers' mess, or whatever they call it in the Navy. It was like being on a holiday cruise. The dining room had tables for four with menus. It was first class.

Our stateroom was big, four to a room. The crossing took nine days, with one stop in Hawaii then on to Yokohama, Japan. Boy, I thought, this is a gentleman's war. I never had accommodations so deluxe in the service before. It was not going to be long, however, before I realized that we were being fattened up for the kill, as the saying goes.

We arrived in Yokohama and boarded a train to Tokyo that was the fastest I had ever been on. Once off the train, we were bused to Camp Drake where we were outfitted for combat. I was given another carbine, though I already had one. I was told to take it. A .45 and holster were also issued, as well as a bayonet. I felt like Rambo.

To make a long story short, within seventy-two hours of docking in Yokohama I was on the ferryboat to Pusan, Korea. In Pusan, I was again in supply and issued another carbine. I told them, "Hell, this makes three. How many can you fire at a time?"

The supply sergeant told me, "There are plenty of guys that can use them where you are going, *sir*."

I was assigned to the 7th Division Artillery, 7th Infantry Division, code name "Bayonet". The arm insignia was the hourglass, as I was to be a forward observer for both air and ground.

The city was a mess with thousands of refugees. Water was a problem. Would you believe that I saw Koreans using water from washing for cooking food? I

171

guess if you boil it, it kills the germs? It was hot and muggy and the place stank of every kind of repugnant odor imaginable. I was here one night and was glad to get out of this decay of human flesh.

One would only have to see this pitiful deterioration of human spirit to understand the stupidity of war. Children begging—all ages, three and up to the teens, for any nourishment. Mud and human excreta was evident everywhere, just filth beyond imagination. The sewers, if there were any, were not working as it was flowing down the streets. The stench was appalling. There were flies by the thousands buzzing and standing stationary on the children's faces and bodies. I thought, hell has to be better that this.

A jeep picked me up. We drove for miles going through the city of Seoul and then north until we arrived at Division Artillery Headquarters, south of Hwachon and north of the 38th parallel. I reported to a major. He looked over my file, noticed that I had been a POW, and was surprised. He commented that they had not been sending former prisoners to Korea. That was all that was said about that. I was informed that I was to report to "C" Battery, 31st Field Artillery.

I said, "The airport is here; why to a field artillery unit?" He explained that at the moment there was a surplus of flyboys and that I needed training as a ground forward observer with an infantry unit to teach me the ropes and procedures. I told him that was a good idea, since I had no idea what 155 mm Howitzer looked like. I also suggested that it might have been a good idea to train me in the States rather than here. He assured me that I would be called back to the airfield soon. For some reason I did not believe him. I was on my way to "C" Battery.

Arriving at the battery the CO asked me questions

about my background. Shaking his head, he commented, "I ask for artillery and they send a fly boy."

I assured him it was not of my choosing and I would be happy to go home if he could arrange it.

He laughed and said, "With a sense of humor like that I am sure you will do just fine. But when you are up on the line, keep your ass down." He went on to tell me that I was the fourth replacement in two months. That was very encouraging; I felt a lot better.

That night I was assigned a cot in the battery artillery fire control tent. In the middle of the night someone yelled, "Fire mission!" A few commands were issued and then all hell broke loose. The tent was maybe fifty yards from the nearest gun and there were six of them. Someone yelled, "Continue fire!"—an artillery term. This went on for a couple of minutes. That was my introduction to the field artillery in a loud noisy way. My thought was, this is not my cup of tea.

I had no idea what the hell I was supposed to do. The next morning the captain told me that I was to relieve the lieutenant on the line attached to an intelligence and recognizance platoon and to report to Lt. Kite. I had a driver and wireless operator assigned and off we went in "my" jeep, so they said. Oh, yes, before I left I told the captain about the three carbines that I had. He said, "Fine. Leave two in supply."

"But I signed for them and they are charged to me, " I replied.

"Hell, there is no accounting for supplies here. Forget it." So I dropped the extra rifles at the supply tent, happy to be rid of them.

We drove up a dirt road and a sign said, "Front Lines". One of the two kids with me said, "This is it, Lieutenant."

"It's what?" I asked.

"This is where we leave the jeep and the lieutenant you are relieving will drive it back. We have to climb this hill to our OP," he answered.

"OP," I said. "What the hell is OP?"

Observation post was the reply. Oh, well, sure, I thought, everyone knows that, wondering what I was to do when I got there, although I was getting a pretty good idea.

The climb up was very difficult and exhausting to the point that you wanted to throw up. Many did and I was not far from it myself. South Koreans and U.S. Infantry occupied the hill and they could tell I was a greenhorn. There were comments like, "Good luck" and "Hey, Lieutenant, after the tenth climb you will run up."

One young soldier said, "Lieutenant, we don't want to lose you. Have a drink. We need you to blow the bastards to hell when they attack tonight." I took the drink with a "Thanks," which was about all I could get out I was so exhausted. We finally did get to the top of this lousy piece of real estate. I was panting so hard, I was so out of shape. I just dropped down and leaned against the bunker. I finally got my wind back. My uniform was soaked through; it was hot and humid. From this vantage point all I could see were ridge lines. I thought, this has to be a foot soldier's nightmare, and more truth than poetry it proved to be.

Meanwhile, Don Moyer, a fellow officer who made the trip with me was attached to the 3rd Division as a forward observer. Don was wounded the first day on the line, a bullet through his buttock. He was taken back to a hospital ship, USS Haven, for repairs and was back to duty after a month or so.

So I met the retread (a World War II veteran) officer

who I was replacing. He informed me that his MOS was a radar officer, and that I should not feel bad, as he knew less than me. He also informed me that the reason for this was that forward observers were being killed faster than they could be trained. This made my day for sure, especially when he said that the observation post, and he pointed, was on the next hill in front of our lines.

Next I met with Lt. Kite, who was officer in charge of the intelligence and reconnaissance platoon. He greeted me with, "Glad to have you aboard." I was not so sure. So he started getting me oriented, and we pored over the maps, Lt. Kite pointing out landmarks and procedures for calling fire missions. I was in direct contact with the battalion fire center. In addition, there was a company of Koreans (Republic of Korea) and two companies of the 7th Infantry. My mission was to search visually and call for artillery fire on everything that moved beyond my position. That was in addition to requests made by air and ground troops. In the event of an enemy attack I was wondering what the hell would happen to us out on the OP—the radio operator, the driver/runner, and me.

The first night we stayed in the OP bunker on the main line. We would fire flares at alternating times to see if there was any activity by the enemy. Thank goodness it was quiet with exception of the occasion artillery shell landing in the vicinity, fired by the North Koreans. Next morning Lt. Kite led the way to the advanced OP. We made our way down the slope diagonally and then doubled back in the valley to try and keep the North Koreans from observing our direction. They obviously had OP posts as well.

The advanced OP was dug into the top of the hill with just a slit on the lea side for the telescope observation. The bunker was large enough for three or four people. The opening had a camouflaged covering made with brush common to the area. We were to stay and observe all day and at night return to the main line following the same path that we used in the morning. The bunker was equipped with a direct telephone line to the division fire center, food and water, a light burp gun (automatic machine gun), and about twenty-five hand grenades.

The view from this point was all narrow ridge hilly terrain; all the trees had been blown to bits from previous artillery pounding. We saw some gooks around noon and I figured I'd get my feet wet. I called a fire mission, one round of phosphorus, then bracket, and fire for effect. That was the drill. It went okay and I felt a little confident. This duty was fourteen days on line and fourteen back with the C Battery. During the first two weeks there was plenty of small action. The gooks would send out feeler squads and I would greet them with fireworks. Nothing big took place, however. If the light aircraft were flying then we would not go to the forward position, because they took over. You would think the plane would be able to spot movement, but in fact the camouflage made it difficult. Ground operation could study areas for hours at a time and detect more.

We were fed one hot meal a day, when possible. It was amazing how those Koreans could make the climb with those big canisters of food for the troops.

I was replaced after fourteen days. The Jeep was at the base of the hill and we drove to the Battery. The weather was miserable, hot and humid. I was dirty after fourteen days and enjoyed a hot shower that was available for the battalion, in a tent, four miles back of the front lines.

Sometime the following day I was to report to headquarters for an indoctrination flight. I drove to the airstrip and this young lieutenant, a few months out of

West Point, was to fly a J-6 to show me the drill. So we took off after briefing, with instructions that we were to maintain 1800 feet above the hilltops to protect us from small arm fire. I did not want to spend another term in a POW camp and flying over enemy territory again made me feel uneasy. So I was told to look sharp and if I saw anything, we would circle to determine if there was a target.

As we were flying, I noticed that we were crossing the hilltops at about 800 feet. I brought it to the attention of the pilot; he assured me it was okay. Well, okay is not okay. We were crossing a ridge line at about 700 feet and bullets were piercing the plane. The engine started coughing and I hollered at the pilot do a one eighty back to our lines, which he did. There was a narrow rutted dirt road in the valley; the plane was hitting on a couple of cylinders and we are too low to bail out.

"Land the damn thing on the road!" I yelled.

"Where?" he asked.

"Anywhere, for Christ's sake," I replied in exasperation.

The road was too narrow, but there was no place else to go, except into the side of a hill. We only had a couple of minutes. He did a good job. We hit in a stall, our speed not more than forty or fifty miles per hour. The wings were torn off and the under carriage snapped in the ruts. We were okay, got out fast, dumped a grenade in the cockpit to destroy radios, and ran like hell.

This was déjà vu for me—not again, I thought, in a POW camp or worse! We were heading in the right direction and were met by our own troops in a Jeep and taken to safety. I can tell you I really gave this lieutenant a piece of my mind. The dumb SOB disregarded the orders and hot-dogging can get you killed or worse as far as I was concerned. A POW again! Back at headquarters in debriefing, however, I lied for the pilot; I told them that we were 1800 feet. I figured he had learned his lesson as he was still shaking the last time I saw him. I never did see him after that. Who knows, maybe he did make the same mistake twice. I hope not.

Summer passed, and the fall season was upon us. We were engaged in the Battle of Heartbreak Ridge and it was during this time that an incredible event took place.

It was a typical day; I was calling artillery missions constantly, for the Marines, Army, both ROK and US. The battle was raging; it was very bloody on both sides. I believe the causalities at Heartbreak Ridge were amongst the highest of the war. The two enlisted men and I were in the usual forward position and the hill was being pounded by Chinese artillery. This usually meant an assault would be forthcoming. Darkness was approaching and I wanted to get out and back to the main line as quickly as possible.

Suddenly the landscape lit up like a Christmas tree and coming up the hill were hundreds of Chinese troops. We had no time to leave without being detected. The flares continued; we put the camouflaged stuffers in the observation slit and at the entry to the bunker. The Chinese came to the top and down the backside of our position into the valley to mount the assault on the main line. Our position was now behind the Chinese and I was requested to call in artillery fire on them. I did and the artillery shell was the kind that exploded thirty feet above the ground, which would be the most effective for this situation. We were okay for that type of shell as we had sufficient protection with the sandbags and the earth above the bunker. The main concern was staying away from the opening to the bunker.

The main line held and the gooks were now coming

back up the hill, dragging wounded and some of their dead. I only saw three or four bodies later on the opposite slope. Anyhow, can you believe that twice we were passed, coming and going, and they did not notice or discover our bunker?

It became very quiet, and we stayed put until daylight. I pulled the camouflaged partition off in the front of the bunker. All was calm; there was no movement. I called control center.

The guy said, "Hey, Lieutenant, you still alive? The major wants you to get the hell back to the main line."

"I'm gone," I replied.

I got back to the main line in time for a hot meal. Remarks were made to us like, "We thought you guys were goners." I did, too. After eating, we were replaced by another cannon fodder lieutenant and I was thinking hot shower.

Winter was setting in and I can tell you Korea was a cold, rotten place for a vacation at that time of year. We were making a lot of military moves, forward and sideways in support of divisions being replaced. The problems were horrendous on the very rugged, hilly, rock-hard, narrow icy roads. The half-tracks that hauled the howitzers and the trucks loaded with supplies slid like they were on ice skates. In the more hilly terrain the curves on the "road" were so sharp that we had trouble navigating around them. We lost more than one that slid over the side of the "road".

Field artillery is never in reserve. If we were not supporting our own 7th division, then it would be other allied units. I was the battery executive officer. Therefore, when I wasn't at the OP, I was moving guns around, placing them in position, and so forth; I was in charge of all the guns.

TWICE SURREAL

The second major battle I was involved in took place north of the 38th parallel, named Yanggu, on the central front. Our division replaced the 1st Marine Division.

I was looking through binoculars. I saw what I thought was a man strung up between two chopped-off trees on top of the hill. It was fully clothed in G.I. fatigues and it was wearing a cap. It moved about and appeared to be a man struggling to get free. Later that evening, Lt. Kite and I, with a handful of soldiers, investigated the "man" and found it to be a scarecrow. It was made of stones and rags in the shape of a human.

The gooks had good reason to do something for protection; artillery had been plastering that hill for days. Fortunately, our only casualty was one of the lads—hit by fragments from an errant artillery round, ours or theirs was the question. His injury was not serious, but enough to get him back to a hospital ship, which I am sure he had no objections to, a nice warm bed and hot food.

Our OP position was with the main force, which I was thankful for. We were pounding every hill in sight. The brass wanted us to get as much territory as possible, due to a rumor that a peace treaty could be in the making. We in turn were the recipients of heavy artillery and one round hit next to our OP bunker, killing the young nineteen-year-old radio operator. So again with heavy losses we regained the ridge line; that was the objective. That's all we ever seem to be fighting for—"ridge lines". Insane, of course, but not in the military mind—you know, "take the high ground".

It was during this time that the one-millionth round of high explosive ammunition was to be fired by the 7th Artillery. It was loaded into the breach of a 155 howitzer of the 31st Field Artillery Battalion, "C" Battery. I was the man in charge of this event. Major General L. L. Lemnitzer, commanding general of the 7th Infantry, pulled the lanyard that sent ninety-seven pounds of destruction on its way to blast another red position.

I believe it was February that I was granted R&R, "rape and rampage", actually rest and recuperation. Had I known how aggravating getting to Japan would be, I would not have gone.

First there was a truck ride, then a train, a plane, and a truck again, each requiring hours of waiting. So it took us thirty-six hours to go 300 miles as the crow flies. We finally ended up at Camp Drake, outside Tokyo. From there I took a cab to the hotel. The weather was cold. I met up with a friend from San Diego; we served in the same unit in San Diego, and also in Washington. His name was Ralph Kulk.

I received a letter from my wife stating that my dad, who was now a real estate broker, arranged financing for my wife to purchase a house in East San Diego, on Vivian Street, in the Rolando Park area. I felt good about the move, as the Poe Street house was small.

The following day I went shopping for the family. What I had left over I would spend for my enjoyment. In a department store I bought a complete set of dishes for twelve, Noritake china. I bought Mikimoto pearl earrings for the girls.

Then Ralph and I opted for hot Japanese bath at the hotel. A steaming tub, without concern, both male and female bathing together. So it did not bother me; I was enjoying the whole scene. We did a few other tourists things and then it was time to return and play war games.

The trip coming back was worse than going out. The seating in the DC-3 that flew us back to Korea was bench style down each side of the fuselage, metal, and it was very cold. We about froze to death just getting back. Then the train ride to Seoul was not much better as lots of the windows were broken or would not close. It was heartbreaking to see these young children begging at the stops we made along the train route. All ages, children with scarcely any clothing and wearing cloth shoes, in sub-zero weather.

All of us (returning soldiers) gave them everything that was available, food, scarves from our necks, jackets, anything we could afford to shed. It was a very pitiful sight, one that remains carved in my memory. The truck that was to take us to our units was canvas covered. This helped the frigid cold of the wind, but it was a miserable night.

On arriving at the battery, about midnight, I was challenged by the sentry on guard. He was standing in a three-sided stand-up sentry box, and he had a small fire burning for warmth. I gave the password, "bayonet". I remarked to him to be careful of the fire and then proceeded towards my tent.

When I was about five paces away from the sentry box, the guard said, "By the way, Lieutenant, your tent burned down while you were away. I was instructed to tell you to sleep in the mess tent tonight." His timing was perfect and after the annoyance wore off I had to chuckle.

It might seem that the fire was insignificant, but most of my personal effects, my favorite jacket, extra clothing, and many other items were lost. Regardless of value, small items become important when they are not easily replaced. So I slept in the mess tent until a new one arrived a few days later. It was so aggravating; I had to fill out a form, explaining the reason in order to get replacement clothing. You will remember they were giving me guns, etc., on the way over without even a signature. Such logic boggles the mind.

When it was necessary to move to another location

we usually did it at night. The reason was to make it more difficult for the Chinese forward observers, and thereby reduce the chances of us being shelled by their artillery. The thrust of this is that on March, 1952, we received orders to relocate our position; we were to move within the hour. It was about 10 am and the location that was assigned was close to the front, closer than usual for 155 Howitzers. I questioned the advisability of this move in daylight.

I was told in no uncertain terms that my advice was not required, and to carry out the orders. With that rebuff, I gave the order to pack up and be ready to move in an hour. The distance was not that great and travel was not difficult as we were traveling up a fairly wide valley. I really felt uncomfortable, as I knew the Chinese were observing us. We were to travel to the first cross road, a wide path, turn left into a valley that was quite narrow— maybe a half-mile wide—and set up.

As I was orienting the guns, we heard the familiar sound, a kind of whistle, which you can't mistake, of artillery incoming. It was white phosphorus exploding long, then one short, and then all hell broke loose; shells were bursting all around us. "Take cover," I yelled. The smell and smoke were so familiar by now. I dove into an irrigation ditch with about a foot of water.

I knew this was going to happen. You couldn't move an artillery unit in the daytime—just the noise of the trucks and half-tracks would wake the dead, besides being observed. The shelling lasted for about half an hour. The casualties were not that high; nine were wounded. The saddest was that the first sergeant, due to be repatriated the following day, was killed. This was very upsetting for all of us. He was tough but fair with the men, well respected, and we worked together compatibly over the last few months. I am certain that had we moved in the darkness this probably would not have happened. In addition to the personnel, two guns and a couple of trucks were beyond repair, as well as other miscellaneous equipment.

I then received an order to head for the high ground and set up an OP, that we were supporting some units from Ethiopia and Turkey. So I left the area, without reservation, and with two enlisted soldiers started another climb, up another 1200 foot mountain, to the front line position.

This is the way it went for the rest of my tour in Korea. I made a few more flights in aircraft and endured a few more battalion relocations, up and down a ton more hills. Finally in July or August 1952, I received orders that my Korean tour was over. I was to report to the seaport at Inchon, for repatriation to Japan and then the United States. The battalion commander asked me to stay another six months, with the promise that I would receive a promotion. I refused for two reasons—my family first, and second, I felt that I had already earned a promotion. I was an efficient officer who carried out all orders. In addition, I was decorated for my actions, being awarded the Bronze Star. A bribe was not going to keep me.

I was anxious to get home but the military is not as fast returning as coming. At the first stop, Inchon, we boarded a landing craft that took us to the ship that would return us to Japan. The ship was anchored about a mile out in the harbor. Hanging off the side were scaling rope ladders, so we had to shoulder strap our duffel bags and climb up the side of the ship to the deck. Quite tricky climbing up I can assure you. The coincidence of this was it was the same ship, the USS General Miegs that had brought me to Yokohama. Even stranger was that I was assigned the same stateroom with the same bed. The chances of that had to be a one in a thousand. I did not think too much about it at the time, but later it occurred to me that it was a "believe it or not" story.

The Miegs took us to Sasebo, Japan. We stayed about a week, and it was a long week since we all wanted to get home. More paper work and medical exams, then we waited. Finally the ship arrived, named USS Carleton. This ship was the same class as the Miegs with all the atmosphere of a cruise ship. On the voyage home we were subjected to personal medical exams daily to check for venereal disease; this would show up in a ten-day crossing.

So it was a very pleasant voyage home and we relaxed on deck and had great meals, served by waiters at tables for four, just like the trip over. Enlisted had very nice accommodations also. Meals were buffet with a fantastic selection.

I had orders to report to a base in El Paso, Texas, after sixty days leave. Leaving Japan the ship was headed for San Francisco, and was to dock at pier 10, with a morning arrival. On arrival travel agents came aboard to help us with transportation to our homes. So I booked a flight to Los Angeles. I called my beloved Bridget and arranged for her to meet me in L.A. and we would stay overnight in Laguna and then drive down to San Diego.

The disembarking in San Francisco was uneventful, not like World War II. No military band was present. People were unconcerned that 58,000 young men lost their lives in the "police action". Most did not even know where Korea was located geographically. I was with three other returnees who had time to kill, like myself, before our air flights took us in different directions. Experiences that we had shared together we would never share again nor would we even see one another again.

So we went into this restaurant and sat down. No one

paid attention to returning veterans anymore, except one. A gentleman approached our table and asked, "You boys just back from Korea?"

We nodded.

He said, "First, I want to welcome you back home and thank you for the sacrifices you have made for us and for the Korean people."

We acknowledged his kind words. He went on to give his name. He told us that he owned the Circus Peanut Company and invited us to see the plant. We questioned him about how long this would take since we had connections to make. As it turned out, we had the time and did visit the plant. He also furnished transportation for us to the airport and all the peanuts and other Circus products we could carry. We were very appreciative of this man, and thanked him profusely, but that was the extent of gratitude shown to us by the United States of America. At that moment, my mind recaptured the filth, bitter cold, mud, and dead comrades. I thought, how could they comprehend?

I was really excited about seeing Bridget, my wife. Funny but I was a little nervous. The plane put down at LAX and I rushed from the plane to meet Biddy. She was nowhere in sight. I immediately was alarmed that something might have happened to her. I was contemplating what to do when I looked over at a young lady sitting and reading a book. I walked over to her and said, "Hello, Biddy." She was so surprised and embarrassed, I think, but she was under the impression that my flight was later. So, with tears, we gathered ourselves together and drove to Laguna and stayed the night after a candlelight dinner.

The following morning we drove to San Diego on Highway 101 and arrived at my parents' home in Point Loma shortly before noon. There to greet me were

Patricia, Susan, and my parents. It was only on my return that I was told of my father's cancer and that he had had an operation for colon cancer, malignant. This was quite a shock to me and although I would not have been able to correct the problem, had I known, the Army would have sent me home. Father seemed in good spirits and he and Mother were planning a trip to Europe in a few months.

We left the parents and drove to the house that I had never seen on Vivian Street. It was nice, but I knew we would not live in that area long.

It was then that I knew it would be better for the family if I requested a discharge from the service. I wrote to Washington for release of my assignment, requesting a discharge, which they granted. I was separated at Camp Cook, now called Vandenberg.

I was recalled to duty when my 746 National Guard Unit was activated to join the U.S Army. Here I am with my beloved wife, Bridget, and daughters Patricia (left) and Susan (right). I am ready to board a train in San Diego at the Santa Fe railroad station to travel to Fort Lewis, Washington for training.

Korea

I am pictured here at Fort Lewis, Washington in 1950 where I subsequently relocated my family.

I was with a training program in Fort Lewis, Washington in 1950.

In the picture above are the "top brass" from Washington D.C. reviewing training programs. I am standing on the right.

This picture was taken in San Diego shortly before I left for Korea. I had returned from Fort Lewis, Washington to get my family resettled once again in San Diego while I would be away in Korea.

TWICE SURREAL

U.S. Naval Ship Gen. M.C. Meigs

I crossed to Japan on the USS General M.C. Meigs.

Ironically, I was assigned the exact same stateroom and bed on a leg of my return trip, from Korea to Japan.

I then sailed on the USS Carlton to San Francisco. I would like to note that the accommodations aboard this ship were excellent.

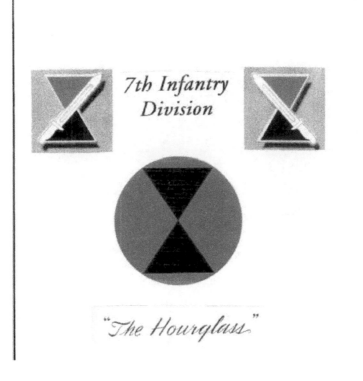

In Korea, I was assigned to the 7th Infantry Division, 31st Field Artillery, Charlie Battery. This was the insignia.

I am pictured here in one of many forward observation bunkers that the forward observers occupied near Hwachon, north of the 38th parallel.

I am at another observation post position. This one is also located north of the 38th parallel in Korea.

I am pictured with Lt. Dickson (right), the motor pool officer, at the front line north of the 38th parallel near Hwachon or Chorwon, Korea in 1951.

Korea

Here are a couple of retreads from WW II. I am on the right with fellow officer, Lt. Walker, in the C Battery camp area.

I am standing next to one of C Battery's 155 Howitzers.

Usually we had four in the squad when we were in a forward position.

Here I am briefing my squad on details of the terrain. I am the second from the right.

A fellow officer and I are shown here eating a typical gourmet meal on the front lines. I'm on the right.

I am clearing an area for relocation. The corpse is of an enemy serviceman.

As we would move into a new area, it was common to clear the surrounding hills.

Lt. Don Moyer (left) and me shipped out to Korea together. We are attending a briefing at the Hwachon reservoir.

This is another picture taken at the Hwachon reservoir.

Here is an example of the 155 Howitzer at full recoil.

The M114 155 mm Howitzer was a towed howitzer used by the United States Army. It was first produced in 1942 as a medium artillery piece under the designation of 155 mm Howitzer M1. It saw service with the US Army during World War II, the Korean War, and the Vietnam War, before being replaced by the M198 howitzer.

This is me wearing my favorite jacket. It was destroyed in the fire while I was on leave in Japan. This jacket was an older issue and it was a treasure.

Colder weather was coming, and we were not equipped, especially in footwear.

I was now working as a Battery Executive Officer. You can see from my clothing how ill equipped the troops were for the frigid weather of Korea.

I am pictured here (right) with 1st Lt. Kilgariff in a staging area. We were getting ready for a battalion move forward. Winter has arrived.

I am pictured here with the infamous one-millionth artillery round to be fired in Korea.

MG Lemnitzer (center) is shown standing in the gun pit where Jan Sterling would fire the one millionth round. I'm to his right.

The 31st Field Artillery Unit, C Battery was chosen to fire the one-millionth artillery round in Korea.

Movie stars arrived including Jan Sterling and her husband Paul Douglas. Jan would have the honor of pulling the lanyard to fire the round (below).

One- millionth round fired by 7th Infantry Artillery, Charlie Battery, Korea on January 23, 1952. (I am next to sign on lower left.)

SCARECROW TRICK TRIED

S. D. Officer Sees Through Red Ruse

ALONG CENTRAL FRONT, Korea, Oct. 18 (Delayed) (UP)—Chinese Communists resorted to a barnyard trick to slow down American artillery fire today.

First Lt. Stuart G. Hunt, of 3551 Poe St., San Diego, serving as forward observer for an artillery unit, said he saw "what I thought was a man strung up between two chopped-off trees on top of the hills.

a man struggling to get free," Hunt said.

Second Lt. Warren A. Kite, a platoon leader from Elizabeth, Pa., investigated the "man" later and found it to be a scarecrow. Kite said it was made of stones and rags in the shape of a human.

"They had good reason to do something for protection," Kite said. "Artillery had been plastering that hill for days."

An article from the San Diego Union newspaper that was also published in The Hourglass magazine.

TWICE SURREAL

The Hourglass — Summer 2008

Stuart Hunt's Korea 1951

Lt. Stuart Hunt Korea 1951

Photos submitted by former 1st Lt. Stuart Hunt, forward observer with Charlie Btry. 31st Field Artillery.

17008 Bernado Oaks Dr., San Diego, CA 92128-2103 eMail: <shunt1@san.rr.com>

Lt. Dicksen (lt) & Lt. Hunt

Lt. Hunt on OP.

U.S. Naval Ship Gen. H.C. Heinz

In the summer of 2008, The Hourglass Magazine published this article about me and the 31st Field Artillery, Charlie Battery 7th Infantry Division, U.S. Army.

EPILOGUE

U pon returning home, I resumed my previous employment with Prudential Insurance Company as a staff manager. Shortly after my return we sold our home and moved near my parents in Point Loma, where Caroline came into the world.

So that was the Stuart and Bridget Hunt family, Patricia, Susan, and Carolyn. The following years were typical family years. The girls married and I have four lovely grandchildren, John Stuart and Susannah Kristine Evans, Matthew Tilden Moschetti, and Genevieve Noelle Gamma. I also have two great-gransons, Cooper Stuart and Spencer John.

My dad died in 1955, at the age of fifty-three. I was at his bedside. Mother died in early 1970 at the age of sixty-six; I was there in her last moments. I had wonderful parents. We were very close and we lived through the good and the bad together.

I worked for Prudential for ten years, Paddock Pools and others for six years. I worked in stock brokerage seventeen or eighteen years. Then Jim Horwood and I owned and manufactured a security product until retirement.

I have been retired now twenty-four and half years and I would like to go back to work to get some time off.

This is the grave of one of our crew members, P/O G.L. Boucher buried in a military cemetery in Holland.

Pictured is the one and only rebuild Halifax Mark III. It is displayed in the Trenton Air Museum in Ontario, Canada. The aircraft was recovered from the bottom of a lake in Norway and rebuilt.

To commemorate the Halifax III at the Trenton Air Museum in Ontario, Canada.

Lightning Source UK Ltd.
Milton Keynes UK
UKHW012049150519
342752UK00003B/26/P